The Comfortable Home

The Comfortable Home

Stylish Ideas for Living

Jessica Elin Hirschman, Candace Ord Manroe, Candie Frankel

MetroBooks

An Imprint of Friedman/Fairfax Publishers

ISBN 1-56799-494-6

Editors: Dana Rosen, Sharyn Rosart, Kelly Matthews, and Hallie Einhorn
Art Director: Jeff Batzli
Designers: Lynne Yeamans and Patrick McCarthy
Photography Editors: Jennifer Crowe McMichael and Emilya Naymark
Photography Director: Christopher C. Bain
Production Manager: Camille Lee

Printed in China by Leefung-Asco Printers Ltd.

10 9 8 7 6 5 4 3 2 1

For bulk purchases and special sales, please contact:
Friedman/Fairfax Publisher
Attention: Sales Department
15 West 26th Street
New York, NY 10010
212/685-6610 FAX 212/685-1307

Visit our website:
http://www.metrobooks.com

TABLE OF CONTENTS

Introduction 8

INTRODUCTION

Opposite: A FINE EXAMPLE OF HOW LESS CAN BE MORE, THIS PORCH SETTING DISPLAYS A BALANCE OF SIMPLICITY AND ELEGANCE THAT COMPLEMENTS BOTH THE TRADITIONAL ARCHITECTURE OF THE HOME AND THE MAGNIFICENT OCEAN VIEW BEYOND.

Anyone going about the business of refeathering the nest knows about the ongoing search for worthy decorating ideas and tips. In the normal course of events, families grow and shrink, and singles strike out on their own. As a result, new rooms are added on and existing rooms become available for new purposes. A home that can hold its own through this revolving door of change is a true treasure, a place where family and friends can feel welcome, sociable, productive, and, alternately, quiet and meditative.

This volume takes a close-up look at four hot spots in today's home. You'll see porches and sunrooms transformed into lush indoor-outdoor living spaces; the family room and its incarnation as den, great room, and recreation room; and bedroom retreats for both adults and children. Unlike formal rooms that are decorated "for show" and used only occasionally, the rooms pictured here are at the hub of family and personal life. In them we read, watch television, snack, talk, debate, study, unwind, play, and hibernate, to name just a few of the many pursuits that occupy our time. Rooms designed for such varied and unpretentious activities must be just as ready to boast physical comfort as they are visual allure.

We instinctively gravitate toward such amenities as comfortable upholstery, the lamp by which to read, and the table on which to set down a beverage glass. When we find that such needs have been anticipated and provided for, we feel much more than instant gratification; we begin to feel at home.

Working out the kinks in a decorating plan will always be part of the interior design challenge. It's critical to create a snarl-free traffic flow, provide ample and appropriate storage, and make the most of low-maintenance products. But the real zest behind any inviting porch, snug family room, or seductive bedroom, as this anthology demonstrates page after page, is unabashed personality. The annotated pictures assembled here rebel against cookie-cutter rooms and bland, faceless furnishings—provided here is a library of advice, inspiration, and designer know-how for turning out rooms with unique profiles. The astute reader will turn to these pages again and again for help in emulating different color schemes, isolating the key furniture and textile components that make up a particular ambience, and analyzing a room's tempo and personality. It would take several years' worth of decorating-magazine subscriptions to garner the wealth of visual ideas and practical advice assembled here. For those who go about decorating one room at a time, the single-subject format is ideal; it concentrates myriad options in one location for easy perusal and reference.

As any interior designer will agree, the well-decorated room looks good, functions smoothly, and always adds up to more than the sum of its parts. Creating a room that lets its inhabitants live and breathe easy is an art worth cultivating, for such rooms, well-conceived, ultimately cast their civilizing influences back on us. Here you will find porches and sunrooms, family rooms and dens, boudoirs and bedrooms that speak a fluent language of comfort, individuality, historicity, sincerity, and passion...and encourage us to do the same.

—Candie Frankel

Opposite: In this converted artist's studio, the separation between inside and outside is as subtle as the green silk curtain that outlines the threshold and complements the room's rich Gothic overtones. A grass matting treatment on the ceiling windows shields the handwoven tapestry upholstery from light and disguises the rough wood window frames. The concrete floor, scored to resemble large bricks, is freshly painted and stenciled for a formal, finished look.

PART ONE

PORCHES & SUNROOMS

JESSICA ELIN HIRSCHMAN

INTRODUCTION

Historically, porches and sunrooms have enjoyed a unique status in residential architecture, bridging the gap between unbounded open space and protected shelter. Today, as the pace of life accelerates and neighborhoods become more and more crowded, a need for open, private living spaces intensifies. The nineties have witnessed a worldwide heightened awareness of the environment, and accompanying this consciousness is a desire to feel a part of nature whenever possible. Porches and sunrooms — transition spaces between inside and outside — address all these desires. These structures, with a long history in residential design, are now undergoing a newfound popularity.

Porches are also called verandas and porticos. Although there are architectural differences among these structures, in the vernacular the terms are generally used interchangeably. Strictly speaking, a porch is

a sheltered entrance, usually a principal entrance, that is permanently attached to and projecting from a building. A veranda is an open, galley-like structure with its own roof and is positioned along the side of a house but not necessarily at its main entrance. Verandas are larger than porches, generally extending the length of the primary elevation and often wrapping around to one or two sides of a house. The word *veranda* came from the Portuguese language via India and entered the Western design lexicon through England.

Opposite: IN THIS CONVERTED ARTIST'S STUDIO, THE SEPARATION BETWEEN INSIDE AND OUTSIDE IS AS SUBTLE AS THE GREEN SILK CURTAIN THAT OUTLINES THE THRESHOLD AND COMPLEMENTS THE ROOM'S RICH GOTHIC OVERTONES. A GRASS MATTING TREATMENT ON THE CEILING WINDOWS SHIELDS THE HANDWOVEN TAPESTRY UPHOLSTERY FROM LIGHT AND DISGUISES THE ROUGH WOOD WINDOW FRAMES. THE CONCRETE FLOOR, SCORED TO RESEMBLE LARGE BRICKS, IS FRESHLY PAINTED AND STENCILED FOR A FORMAL, FINISHED LOOK. Above: HISTORICALLY, THE DESIGN AND FURNISHING OF A FRONT PORCH WAS AN INTEGRAL STRUCTURAL AND AESTHETIC ELEMENT OF A HOME'S FAÇADE. THE PILLARS OF THIS PORCH REFLECT THE INFLUENCE OF GREEK REVIVAL ARCHITECTURE. THE ELEVATED SEATING AREA IS FURNISHED IN A POPULAR COUNTRY STYLE.

Porticos are long, formal, symmetrical porches derived from classical Greek architecture. The portico is protected overhead by a triangular gable or pediment roofline that is supported by columns. Porticos traditionally were designed to shelter main entrances but over time were moved to the sides of buildings, especially churches, to protect secondary entrances and egresses.

Originally, one of the primary functions of the porch was to help cool a house. In warm climates where passive solar cooling was essential, homes often featured a second-story porch to allow the circulation of breezes. Extensive roof overhangs also helped cool interior rooms by shading the porch. And on very hot nights, the porch often doubled as a makeshift bedroom.

Particularly in warm climates, the function of the porch was expanded into the social arena (in cold, less hospitable regions, it functioned mainly as temporary shelter from inclement weather). As porches grew in size and boasted more elaborate designs, they became gathering spots and served as prime vantage points over daily neighborhood happenings or surrounding vistas. In agrarian societies, porches often formed the dividing line between work (outside) and play (inside). These in-between spaces were the resting place for dirty shoes and work clothes.

Once air conditioning became widespread, porches were slowly abandoned in favor of cooler, more comfortable interiors. Today, however, residential design is witnessing a revival of the porch. A growing fondness for homes that strike a nostalgic chord is causing many people to return to architecture reminiscent of their

Above: IN COLD CLIMATES, PORCHES OFFER TEMPORARY RESPITE FROM INCLEMENT WEATHER. THIS SHED-STYLE PORCH ON A STONE CABIN ALSO PROVIDES DRY, ACCESSIBLE FIREWOOD STORAGE. TABLE AND CHAIRS ALLOW THE PORCH TO BE FULLY ENJOYED ON WARM DAYS.

Above: FILLED WITH A VARIETY OF FLOWERING PLANTS, THIS OPEN-AIR PORCH REINFORCES AN OUTDOORS ATMOSPHERE WHILE PROVIDING THE COMFORTS OF SEATING AND SHELTER.

parents' or grandparents' homes. For some, that might mean the inclusion of a front or back porch; for others it entails a different type of indoor/outdoor space such as a sunroom or conservatory.

By definition, a sunroom is a room that receives a lot of sun; it might be a freestanding, all-glass structure or an enclosed porch with floor-length windows and skylights. Although *solarium, sun space,* and *conservatory* are all commonly accepted terms for sunrooms, there are differences between a sunroom and an authentic English-style conservatory.

The term *conservatory* dates back to England in the eighteenth century, when "conservative walls" were erected to facilitate the growing of fruit. These walls were actually the combination of two separate structures, one solid—most likely brick or stone—and the other a frame of glass that was placed a few feet in front of the solid wall. The resulting narrow, partially sheltered plot of land became the fruit garden. The concept of the conservatory as an independent structure, however, is even older.

Botanical gardens, extremely popular in sixteenth-century Europe, arrived in England around the year 1620 but did not weather the British climate very well. By the end of the century, an inspired gardener had come up with the idea of constructing a glass building to harbor the delicate plants through the winter months. As the British developed a penchant for exotic fruits such as lemons and oranges, these seasonal havens became known as orangeries. Generally composed of a glass roof and glass wall panels, orangeries were used to display and cultivate the tender fruit plants, and eventually

Opposite: TRADITIONAL ENGLISH CONSERVATORIES BEGAN AS WINTER HARBORS FOR DELICATE, EXOTIC FRUITS AND HAVE EVOLVED INTO LIVING AREAS THAT STRIKE A GRACIOUS BALANCE BETWEEN INDOOR AND OUTDOOR SPACE. THE GLAMOROUS INTERIOR OF THIS FREESTANDING CONSERVATORY WAS CAREFULLY DESIGNED TO REFLECT AND REFRACT LIGHT. A FACETED CHANDELIER BOUNCES THE SUN'S RAYS ACROSS THE VAULTED GLASS CEILING, WHILE SILVER-LEAFED GLASS CABOCHONS REFLECT LIGHT UPWARD FROM THE ELEGANT FLOOR. EVEN THE SKIRTING OF THE TERRY CLOTH RECLINING SOFA POSSESSES TINY, DAZZLING CRYSTALS. THE CLASSICALLY STYLED CHAIR AND EARLY NINETEENTH-CENTURY BRONZE TABLE BRING THE EXCLUSIVE ELEGANCE OF AN ITALIAN PALACE TO THIS GARDEN HIDEAWAY.

heating and lighting systems were added to better control the indoor climate. Edwardians appropriately termed the glass structures "winter gardens."

Conservatories came into their own architecturally, too. Designing and constructing glass buildings was elevated to an art form, and ornamentation signifying wealth and stature became the conservatory's hallmark. Conservatories not only housed horticulture; they extended the living space and brought light into England's interiors during damp winter months.

In terms of both design and popularity, the English conservatory achieved its apogee in the late nineteenth century, but with a growing disfavor of things Victorian suffered a decline during the early twentieth century. But these unique buildings would endure and enjoy newfound popularity in and far beyond England in later years.

Residential design for the 1990s is moving back to basics. Sunrooms and conservatories make it possible to live close to nature and create a sense of openness without compromising the need to be protected and

sheltered. These structures are an economical way to improve a home, as they are viable for use as breakfast rooms, home offices, or mini-kitchens. They can also be designed to serve as a breezeway between garage and house or to link an existing structure to an addition. Topping a townhouse with a conservatory will add a bonus floor of warm, accessible living space.

How the sun space is used may determine its position. Southern exposures are best for capturing the most daylight but may be too hot in warm climates. In cool regions, siting a conservatory on a true east-west axis will allow it to collect heat throughout most of the day. Aligning the structure with a specific view is also an option. A conservatory or sunroom must be able to withstand local weather, and how it will be used will determine its heating, cooling, and lighting systems.

The following chapters contain beautiful examples of porches, sunrooms, and other spaces that, although technically neither porch nor sunroom, illustrate the extent to which architecture can reconcile the need for shelter with the desire for open space.

Opposite: IN WARM CLIMATES, OPEN-AIR PORCHES PROVIDE A ROMANTIC SETTING FOR DINING OUTDOORS.

PORCHES

"The porch is a great social device," explains Robert Davis, developer of Seaside, a planned community in Florida that seeks to recapture the bygone era of small-town living. "Even if unoccupied, porches present a friendly face to the street." Elizabeth Plater-Zyberk, who along with partner Andres Duany developed the master town plan for Seaside, points out that porches are occupants' connection to the street. "On a porch it's possible to be in a private space and still participate in a public sense — and the public can participate in a home-owner's private world."

The boundaries between private and public realms can be intentionally blurred by the design of a porch.

Architectural details or furnishings often set the tone of the space, just as design and decoration establish the mood of an interior room. Not only is the porch an extension of the living spaces, it is often the first element of a home that visitors see. The following photographs present ideas for enjoying the private, the public, the formal, and the relaxed pleasures of a porch.

Opposite: THE RENTAL HONEYMOON COTTAGES AT THE PLANNED COMMUNITY OF SEASIDE, FLORIDA, FEATURE TWO DISTINCT PORCHES. THE GROUND-LEVEL PORCH, WHICH CONNECTS TO THE BEDROOM, IS SCREENED IN FOR PRIVACY. THE SECOND-STORY PORCH OFF THE LIVING ROOM IS OPEN TO TAKE ADVANTAGE OF THE STUNNING VISTA. THESE DOUBLE-STORY PORCHES ARE CAPPED WITH A GALVANIZED METAL ROOF AND HAVE WOOD FLOORING THAT HAS BEEN BLEACHED FOR A COOL, FRESH LOOK. Above left: THE SLIGHT OPENING BETWEEN THE RAILING AND PORCH FLOOR FACILITATES THE DRYING OF THE WOOD AFTER RAIN. Above right: ARCHITECT LEON KRIER'S HOME AT SEASIDE IS A FOUR-STORY TOWERLIKE STRUCTURE WITH SEVERAL PORCHES. THE RAILING IS A UNIQUE DESIGN BUT THE EXPOSED RAFTER CEILING MATCHES THOSE OF SURROUNDING PORCHES.

Above: A portico pays homage to its Greek heritage with a contemporary twist. Fine round columns frame the door in a classical manner, but their asymmetrical placement adds a surprising, distinctive rhythm to the home's front façade. **Opposite:** Reminiscent of a Greek temple, the columned porch on this private residence is technically a veranda because it extends beyond the home's entrance; verandas generally run the length of a front elevation and wrap around the side of a house. Often, however, local vernacular rather than adherence to architectural definitions determines the popular name of a porch. The absence of railings makes this porch feel even more open and spacious.

Opposite: ON THIS PORCH, A CASUAL COMBINATION OF COLOR, STYLE, AND FLORA ENHANCES A SHINGLE-STYLE HOME. CHINTZ PILLOWS AND A HANDCRAFTED RUG DECORATE THE ARRANGEMENT IN EASY-GOING COMFORT. **Top left:** A CAREFUL BALANCE OF INDOOR AND OUTDOOR ELEMENTS GIVES THIS PORCH A WELCOMING SPIRIT. THE INCORPORATION OF SIDE-BY-SIDE SKYLIGHTS AND THE PREDOMINANT USE OF WHITE—INCLUDING AN OFF-WHITE AREA RUG PLACED ATOP THE WHITE-PAINTED FLOORBOARDS—UNIFY THE SPACE AND MAKE IT FEEL LIKE AN INTIMATE LIVING ROOM. **Bottom left:** BLUE STAIRS AND FLOOR, WHICH FEATURES A HAND-PAINTED OLD-FASHIONED COMPASS, MAKE THIS BACK-DOOR PORTICO EVOCATIVE OF A FRONT PORCH FROM THE 1920S. THE SOLID-BLUE ACCENT PILLOWS APPEAR TUFTED BUT ARE ACTUALLY TROMPE L'OEIL CHINTZ.

Above: SCULPTED RAILS HARMONIZE WITH GREEK COLUMNS, BEFITTING THE PALATIAL FEEL OF A PORCH WITH A COMMANDING VIEW. **Near right:** THE PORCH OF THIS HILLSIDE CABIN FEATURES A CUSTOM-DESIGNED RAILING THAT ECHOES THE SHAPE OF THE SURROUNDING TREES. THE RAILING'S BROWN-STAINED "BRANCHES" TOPPED WITH GREEN REINFORCE THE IMAGE. BOTH THE RAILING AND WAVY PINE CHAIRS RECALL THE TURN-OF-THE-CENTURY ARTS AND CRAFTS DESIGN MOVEMENT. **Far right:** A CLASSIC RAILING ON A PORCH IN CAROLLING, FLORIDA, REFLECTS THE REGIONAL CREOLE STYLE OF ARCHITECTURE. THE RAILING CAP IS SLIGHTLY SLOPED, AS IS THE FLOOR, TO FACILITATE WATER RUNOFF.

Opposite: THE SECOND-STORY GABLE, WHICH WAS BADLY CHARRED IN THE FIRE, WAS REPRODUCED RIGHT DOWN TO THE HORSESHOE-SHAPED ARCH THAT WAS THE FASHION AT THE TIME THE HOUSE WAS BUILT. A NEW, HISTORICALLY CORRECT FINIAL CROWNS THE TURRET SHELTERING THE LEFT END OF THE PORCH. **Below:** BOYER AND JOHNSON WORKED TEN YEARS ON THE PROJECT, SELECTING KILN-DRIED REDWOOD FOR THE STRUCTURAL ELEMENTS, INCLUDING THE BALUSTRADES AND NEWEL POSTS OF THE FRONT STAIRS.

INTRICATE, ELABORATE PORCHES WERE A HALLMARK OF VICTORIAN STICK-STYLE AND QUEEN ANNE HOMES. THIS GRAND EXAMPLE OF QUEEN ANNE ECLECTIC IS ACTUALLY A COMPLETE RENOVATION, PAINSTAKINGLY UNDERTAKEN BY HOMEOWNERS JUDY BOYER AND JOE JOHNSON AFTER A FIRE DESTROYED THE HOME'S SECOND STORY. **Above:** A PHOTOGRAPH FROM THE INTERIOR OF THE PORCH PROVIDES A CLOSE VIEW OF THE REFURBISHED ORIGINAL LATTICEWORK AND THE MOON ARCHES—A DETAIL THAT BOYER BELIEVES WAS DERIVED FROM THE INFLUENCE OF THE ORIENTAL SHIPPING TRADE. THE STRAIGHT-GRAIN CEDAR FLOORING WAS PAINTED AN AUTHENTIC SHADE OF GRAY, WHILE THE WILLIAMSBURG BLUE CEILING IS IN KEEPING WITH PHOTOGRAPHS FROM THE PERIOD.

Left: AN EXAGGERATED OVERHANG ADDS A DEFINITE SENSE OF ENCLOSURE TO THIS PORCH. THE RED AND YELLOW STRIPES SET OFF THE CEILING AND CREATE THE ILLUSION OF A PARTIAL WALL.

Below: THIS UNUSUALLY LARGE, ROUND PORCH IS THE PERFECT SETTING FOR PAMPERED INDOOR/OUTDOOR LIVING. THE FABRIC-WRAPPED CEILING, BALLOON SHADES, AND FORMAL DRAPES MAKE THE ROOM FEEL LIKE A ROMANTIC, CANOPIED CAROUSEL. THE VIEW, THE POTTED PLANTS, AND THE WICKER FURNITURE ARE THE ONLY REMINDERS THAT THIS IS A PORCH. SEE-THROUGH PLASTIC SHEETS SHELTER THE ROOM FROM THE ELEMENTS BUT CAN BE RAISED TO LET IN AIR.

DECORATING A PORCH CAN BE AS PERSONAL AS ACCESSORIZING ANY OTHER PART OF THE HOUSE. DIFFERENT ROOF STRUCTURES AND CEILING TREATMENTS HELP SHAPE THE CHARACTER OF THESE PORCHES.

Opposite: EXPOSED HARDWOOD RAFTERS APPEAR NATURAL AND UNPRETENTIOUS ON THIS PORCH WITH MINIMAL DETAILS. THE PITCHED ROOF HELPS SHADE THE PORCH, WHILE LOUVERED DOORS ALLOW BREEZES TO CIRCULATE THROUGH THE ADJACENT INTERIOR SPACES WITHOUT COMPROMISING PRIVACY.

Top right: ARTFUL INTERPRETATIONS OF TIMELESS ADIRONDACK CHAIRS SUIT THE CONTEMPORARY FEEL OF THIS COLORFUL FLAGSTONE PATIO. THE RANDOM, UNEVENLY SHAPED BURSTS OF RED, GRAY, AND BLUE CONTRAST WITH THE STUCCO HOUSE, MAKING THE PATIO FLOOR APPEAR AS WALL-TO-WALL PATTERNED CARPET.

Bottom right: FURNITURE CAN ESTABLISH THE PERSONALITY OF AN OUTDOOR SPACE. HERE, A RUSTIC TABLE AND CHAIRS SET THE MOOD FOR ALFRESCO DINING ON AN ELEVATED PORCH. THE FURNISHINGS ARE PATTERNED AFTER THE TWIG FURNITURE MADE POPULAR IN THE AMERICAN SOUTH—IT WAS MOST OFTEN CONSTRUCTED OF HICKORY BECAUSE OF THE WOOD'S EXCEPTIONAL ABILITY TO WEATHER HEAT AND HUMIDITY. UPHOLSTERED THROW PILLOWS CUSHION THE SLAT SEATS AND COMPLEMENT THE VINE-WRAPPED CORNERPOSTS AND RAILING.

Right: AT THE OPPOSITE END OF THE ABOVE PORCH, A WICKER SETTEE AND OVERSIZED ARMCHAIR WITH A WARM TOBACCO FINISH PROVIDE THE PERFECT OUTDOOR GROUPING FOR A CASUAL CONVERSATION OR AFTERNOON TEA. THE HOOKED RUG AND WICKER TRUNK USED AS A COFFEE TABLE GIVE THE PORCH A LIVED-IN FEELING.

BUILT AS PART OF AN ADDITION TO
THE NORTH SIDE OF THIS 1920S
HOUSE, THIS PORCH FUNCTIONS
AS A NATURALLY COOL LIVING
SPACE IN THE SUMMERTIME.

Left: ARRANGED TO MIMIC AN
ORIENTAL RUG, THE BLUE AND
GREEN TILES OF THE FAMILY ROOM
FLOOR REFLECT THE NATURAL
PALETTE SURROUNDING THE HOME.
SKYLIGHTS HELP DISTRIBUTE LIGHT
EVENLY THROUGHOUT THE PORCH.

Right: THIS ELEVATED PORCH
HAS THE FEEL OF A TREEHOUSE.
LATTICEWORK BETWEEN THE
SUPPORTS CREATES THE ILLUSION
OF A FLOATING PORCH.

Left: THE USE OF PLYWOOD
CUTOUTS WAS A POPULAR
DESIGN TECHNIQUE IN THE ARTS
AND CRAFTS MOVEMENT OF
THE EARLY TWENTIETH CENTURY.
HERE, MATISSE- AND ARP-
INSPIRED SHAPES CAST DYNAMIC,
EVOCATIVE PATTERNS OF
SHADOW AND LIGHT ACROSS
THE FLOOR.

FLOORING MATERIALS ARE EFFECTIVE DESIGN TOOLS FOR PERSONALIZING A PORCH
AND BLURRING THE BOUNDARIES BETWEEN INTERIOR AND EXTERIOR SPACE. **Above:** THE
PATTERN OF LARGE GREEN AND WHITE FLOOR TILES SHOWN HERE WOULD BE EQUALLY
APPROPRIATE IN A GRAND FOYER. THIS RAMBLING, WELL-SHADED VERANDA RECALLS THOSE
OF THE CARIBBEAN, WITH CHIPPENDALE-INSPIRED, CUSTOM-DESIGNED CHAIRS AND
SETTEE GIVING IT A TIMELESS ELEGANCE. THE RAILING IS COMPRISED OF VASE-SHAPED,
PRECAST CONCRETE BALUSTERS; SMALLER, SCALED-DOWN VERSIONS COULD EASILY ADORN
AN INTERIOR STAIRCASE. **Right:** SIMPLE, NATURAL MATERIALS ARE PERFECT FOR
PORCHES WITH A VIEW. TERRA-COTTA TILES AND WOOD SUPPORTS PAINTED A RICH GREEN
GIVE THIS PORCH AN ORGANIC FEEL THAT SUITS THE ROLLING AUSTRALIAN LANDSCAPE.

As a quiet place for introspection, a porch can carry people away to another time and place. The right appointments can transport one to a world of opulence and indulgence. **Left:** This sumptuous porch features weather-resistant materials and furnishings, including an exquisite handwoven hammock from South America. The custom trompe l'oeil painting on the plaster ceiling, the rich floor tiles, and the white sailcloth drapes bordered with green-and-white striped diamonds give the porch the quality of a finished indoor room. By contrast, matching statues and flowering plants befitting a formal garden add an outdoor, botanical air. **Above:** Although distinctively set apart by its grand rotunda shape and elegantly stenciled floor, this porch appears to be connected to the lawn by virtue of the shared colors. Green and white curtains sewn from the same fabric that covers the wrought-iron chairs bring a soft sense of enclosure and cohesiveness to the space. Small touches, such as tasseled pull cords and fanciful wrought-iron planters, add to the formal character of the space.

SUNROOMS & CONSERVATORIES

Sunrooms and conservatories recall a different place and time, a romantic era when house and garden came together within a room of glass. Originally developed in Britain to sustain the growth of exotic fruits, these glass structures were soon filled with varieties of lush foliage and inviting furnishings.

Today, these structures are enhanced by climate-control technologies and construction materials. The development of energy-efficient thermal glass, ultraviolet-reflective window coverings, attractive heat-absorbing tiles, and fade-resistant upholstery has made it feasible to open all homes to the outside.

Architecturally, the distinction between true conservatories and sunrooms is by some accounts subtle and by others great. The difference lies in the roof. Traditional conservatory roofs come in three architectural styles: the ogee, which is an S-shape crowned with a finial; the vault, which resembles a slightly arched dome; and the classic gable roof design. Sunroom roofs, by contrast, are often designed to blend with the roofline of the house rather than stand apart as a distinct architectural structure. Furthermore, traditional conservatories were constructed entirely of glass, whereas the modern-day sunroom can incorporate other building materials.

The photos featured on the following pages present the warm, welcoming world of many types of glass-room additions.

Opposite: THE BRIGHT PINK, UNIQUELY SHAPED BALCONY AND CIRCULAR STAIRWELL OF THIS GLASS-AND-STEEL-TOPPED SITTING ROOM GIVE THE IMPRESSION THAT IT IS OUTSIDE. INDUSTRIAL OUTDOOR LIGHTING, FRENCH DOORS TRIMMED WITH LACE CURTAINS, AND THE PRESENCE OF THE SKY, VISIBLE THROUGH THE GLASS ROOF, REINFORCE THE IMAGE OF AN EXTERIOR FAÇADE. **Above:** ORIGINALLY A GREENHOUSE, THIS TRADITIONAL ENGLISH CONSERVATORY HAS BEEN CONVERTED INTO AN ARTIST'S STUDIO. IT NOW FEATURES MANUALLY CONTROLLED CANVAS SHADES FOR ADJUSTING THE LIGHTING AND MINIMIZING SOLAR BUILDUP ON HOT AFTERNOONS.

Above: THE INTERIOR OF THIS WHITE-FRAMED CONSERVATORY HAS BEEN ADROITLY FURNISHED BY THE HOMEOWNER, AN ANTIQUES DEALER AND CONSUMMATE FURNITURE COLLECTOR. WINDOWS CAN BE OPENED AND CLOSED INDEPENDENTLY TO DIRECT THE FLOW OF AIR THROUGH THE SPACE OR BREAK A HARSH WIND. **Left:** THE SMALL TRELLIS IS AN ATTRACTIVE, UNOBTRUSIVE WAY TO WRAP THE QUAINT SPACE IN GREENERY. **Right:** INSIDE THE CONSERVATORY, THE VIVID YELLOW WALL REFLECTS SUNLIGHT, MAKING THE SMALL ROOM APPEAR LARGER AND BRIGHTER.

Opposite: CREAM SILK JACQUARD CURTAINS SWAGGED GENTLY ACROSS THE WINDOWS GIVE THIS VAULTED CONSERVATORY A MYSTERIOUS ALLURE. DELICATE TOPIARY CHAIRS ON EITHER SIDE OF THE INVITING ENTRANCE ADD TO THE ENCHANTMENT.

Above: SET AGAINST THE EVENING SKY AND BACKLIT BY AN ADJACENT ROOM, THIS ROUND CONSERVATORY RESEMBLES A ROMANTIC, GLASS-ENCLOSED VICTORIAN PARLOR OR A JEWEL BOX CROWNED WITH A FINIAL.

Above: SUNROOMS ARE PARTICULARLY POPULAR IN COLD CLIMATES, WHERE THE WEATHER PROHIBITS YEAR-ROUND OUTDOOR LIVING. BENT WILLOW AND OTHER COLONIAL FURNISHINGS ARE JUST RIGHT FOR A SUNROOM ADDITION TO A STONE FARMHOUSE. **Right:** IN SOME REGIONS, SUNROOMS ARE SYNONYMOUS WITH SOLARIUMS; BOTH ARE GLASSED-IN ROOMS EXPOSED TO THE SUN. THIS ALUMINUM-FRAMED SOLARIUM CONTAINS A FULLY EQUIPPED KITCHEN WITH DINING AREA FOR YEAR-ROUND "OUTDOOR" ENTERTAINING. SMALLER WINDOWS NEAR THE GOURMET RANGE OPEN TO VENTILATE THE SPACE.

ALTHOUGH NOT PREDOMINENTLY ENCLOSED
BY GLASS, THESE LOVELY ROOMS STILL FEEL OPEN TO
NATURE. **Above:** ISRAELI SCULPTRESS ILANA
GOOR'S LIVING ROOM, WITH HIGHLY POLISHED
ISRAELI STONE FLOORING AND FURNISINGS OF HER
OWN DESIGNS, OVERLOOKS THE MEDITERRANEAN
SEA. **Left:** BAMBOO FURNITURE, A HERRINGBONE-
PATTERNED BRICK FLOOR, AND PAINTED BRICK
WALLS GIVE THIS FULLY ENCLOSED ROOM A CASUAL,
OUTDOOR CHARACTER. **Right:** A SPECTACULAR
PANORAMIC VIEW IS SEEN THROUGH THE
FLOOR-TO-CEILING WINDOWS AND FRENCH DOORS
IN THE MAIN ROOM OF THIS WEEKEND HOME.

Left: This small conservatory located off the library of the Mark Twain House in Hartford, Connecticut, reflects the architectural heritage of the conservatory as greenhouse. A simple shade is the only physical boundary between the two rooms and can be easily maneuvered from either side. **Above:** A glass ceiling of a semi-enclosed London porch gives it the look and feel of a conservatory. Built in Edwardian times, this indoor/outdoor room serves as an extension of the main living space. The climbing vines turn the porch into a private arbor.

Left: WRAPAROUND WINDOWS FLOOD THE SMALL SUNROOM WITH LIGHT AND WARMTH THROUGHOUT THE DAY, AND A HIGH SLOPING CEILING MAKES IT FEEL EVEN MORE OPEN AND AIRY. THE SLATE BORDER IS AN ATTRACTIVE, LOW-MAINTENANCE PERIMETER USEFUL FOR WATERING PLANTS. SLATE ALSO PAVES THE PATIO OUTSIDE, CREATING THE ILLUSION OF UNINTERRUPTED SPACE.

Right: THE SALTBOX ROOFLINE OF THIS COLONIAL HOME FACILITATED THE ADDITION OF A SUNROOM AND FLANKING ALCOVES, WHICH HOUSE A WET BAR ON THE RIGHT AND BUILT-IN BOOKSHELVES ON THE LEFT. FRENCH DOORS CONNECT BOTH ENDS OF THE ADDITION TO THE OUTSIDE.

Left: ALTHOUGH STYLED TO LOOK OLD, THE FARMHOUSE IS ACTUALLY NEW, BUILT FROM MATERIALS COLLECTED OVER A TEN-YEAR PERIOD. MOTORIZED AWNINGS ON THE CEILING AND WALLS SHADE THE SUN-ROOM DURING THE SUMMER.

Right: THIS L-SHAPED SUNROOM, DESIGNED FOR YEAR-ROUND LIVING, FUNCTIONS AS THE SOLE PASSAGEWAY BETWEEN A MANOR HOUSE AND A BARN STRUCTURE, WHICH IS THE HOME'S GREAT ROOM. MEXICAN QUARRY TILES FASHIONABLY CONCEAL A COIL HEATING SYSTEM LOCATED UNDER THE FLOOR, AND VICTORIAN-STYLE VENTS COVER THE AIR CONDITIONING DUCTS LOCATED NEAR THE TRACK LIGHTING. OLD COPPER LANTERNS—EACH ONE DIFFERENT AND ALL ELECTRIFIED—ILLUMINATE THE SPACE AT NIGHT.

Left: A SWEEPING VIEW OF THE INTERIOR REVEALS THE ROOM'S ECLECTIC CHARACTER, REPLETE WITH ENGLISH REGENCY AND GOTHIC FURNISHINGS. THE PROMINENTLY DISPLAYED BIRD CAGE IS AN AUTHENTIC CHINESE CHIPPENDALE DESIGN. THE TILED FLOOR AND MOTORIZED CANVAS WINDOW COVERINGS ARE THE ONLY VISIBLE REMINDERS OF MODERN-DAY LIVING.

THIS ELEGANT, INVITING ROOM IS ACTUALLY A ROOFTOP CONSERVATORY. **Opposite:** LIGHT ENTERS THIS CORNER OF THE ROOM FROM THREE LEVELS: THE GLASS ROOF, THE CEILING-HEIGHT STAINED-GLASS WINDOWS, AND A SMALL FLAT SKYLIGHT POSITIONED DIRECTLY ABOVE THE COUCH. GOTHIC-STYLE TWISTING COLUMNS DEFINE THE COVERED SEATING AREA. **Right:** THE DRAMATIC ENTRYWAY RESEMBLES THAT OF A FORMAL GARDEN, COMPLETE WITH A GATELIKE DOOR, LATTICE-COVERED WALLS, AND ART NOUVEAU STATUES.

Right: THE THOUGHTFUL APPLICATION OF WEDGWOOD BLUE PAINT TO THE INTERIOR AND EXTERIOR OF THIS ENGLISH CONSERVATORY GIVES THE ARCHITECTURE A PLAYFUL LOOK SUITABLE FOR A CONTEMPORARY HOME. ALTHOUGH SUBTLE, THE COLOR IS EVIDENT ENOUGH TO DISTINGUISH THE STRUCTURE FROM ITS FORMAL GARDEN SETTING. **Below:** ALTHOUGH THE SLOPING ROOFLINE OF THIS CONSERVATORY IS CONTEMPORARY, THE PREDOMINANT USE OF WHITE ALUMINUM AND THE BRICK BASE LEND IT A TOUCH OF TRADITIONALISM. TRUE TO THE DESIGN OF AN AUTHENTIC CONSERVATORY, THE SPACE MAY BE ENTERED FROM THE INSIDE OR THE OUTSIDE OF THE HOUSE.

Opposite: ALTHOUGH TYPICALLY FABRICATED IN VICTORIAN OR GOTHIC STYLES, CONSERVATORIES CAN BE CUSTOM-DESIGNED TO COMPLEMENT ANY ARCHITECTURE. THE GLASS ADDITION TO THIS FARMHOUSE WAS DESIGNED IN THE REGENCY STYLE. FROM A DISTANCE, THE FEATHERY LOOK OF THE CONSERVATORY'S ALUMINUM AND GLASS STRUCTURAL COMPONENTS GIVES THE HOUSE A SOLID YET GRACEFUL APPEARANCE.

Outdoor Structures & Spaces

Articulating the relationship between interior and exterior, renowned architect Miës Van der Rohe stated: "The window is a wall, a screen a garden." Swiss-born modern architect Le Corbusier, a master of the manners in which design articulates space, conceptualized space as continuous rather than finite and bounded, considering basic structures such as walls to be mediators, not barriers.

The rooms, structures, and spaces featured on the following pages exemplify how today's architecture interprets the ideas of Van der Rohe, Corbusier, and other innovative architects concerning inside and outside space. The projects all fall under the general heading of "outdoor spaces" but each examines the issue of how to blur boundaries in an individual way.

Some projects take a subtle approach, others strongly deemphasize the traditional definitions of indoor and outdoor. Still others actually invert the concept through the clever use of a cabana, a gazebo, or removable glass panels. They are all included in this book about porches and sunrooms for their ingenuity— and for their ability to reexamine the relationship between shelter and exposure, between indoor and outdoor spaces, and between private and public realms.

Opposite: By establishing visual and physical boundaries, outdoor structures define exterior spaces just as walls delineate interior ones. This thoughtfully designed, open wood frame contrasts with the solidly enclosed spaces of the adjoining house. The structure, built from Douglas fir, was painted green to blend with surrounding foliage. Above: A broadly scaled trellis serves as a roof of sorts to this tropical courtyard. Caribbean colors decorate the space, and arched portals provide a glimpse of the garden beyond.

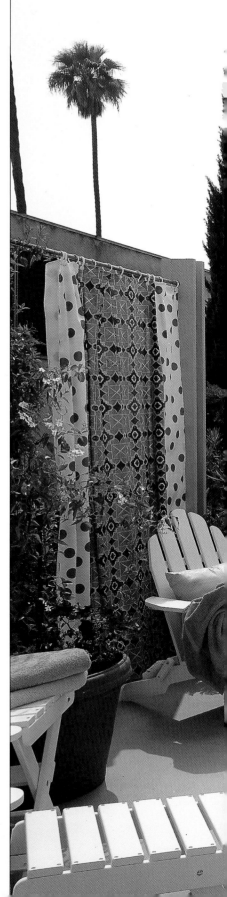

HERE, AS IN NOMADIC TRADITION, TEXTILES SERVE AS THE ONLY BOUNDARIES SURROUNDING PRIVATE

OUTDOOR LIVING SPACES. **Above:** THE IMAGINATIVE USE OF A SOFTLY PATTERNED PASTEL CURTAIN IN PLACE

OF CONVENTIONAL SCREENS TURNS A SIMPLE DECK INTO A LOVELY BILLOWING HIDEAWAY. OVERSIZED

PILLOWS EVOKE THE AMBIENCE OF A RICHLY APPOINTED ARABIAN TENT. **Right:** THE IMAGINATIVE OWNER OF

THIS HOME TURNED A GARAGE-TOP PATIO INTO A WHIMSICAL ROOM FOR OUTDOOR ENTERTAINING.

Left: THIS GAZEBO, A FRENCH COUNTRY STRUCTURE THAT FEATURES A CEDAR SHAKE ROOF AND DOUGLAS FIR COMPONENTS, WAS ASSEMBLED ON SITE FROM A KIT. **Below:** THE MILLED REDWOOD FLOOR IN THIS PREFABRICATED GAZEBO IS DESIGNED TO LOOK LIKE INDIVIDUAL BRICKS BUT IS ACTUALLY ONE UNIT THAT FOLDS IN HALF FOR EASY INSTALLATION.

A GAZEBO IS A FREESTANDING, ROOFED STRUCTURE THAT IS GENERALLY ROUND OR OCTAGONAL AND IS OPEN ON ALL SIDES. HISTORICALLY, GAZEBOS AND GARDEN HOUSES ENJOYED A UNIQUE STATUS, PARTICULARLY IN FORMAL GARDENS, WHERE THEY FUNCTIONED AS A SPOT FROM WHICH TO APPRECIATE THE COLORFUL, MANICURED SCENERY AND BECAME AN INTEGRAL PART OF THE GARDEN DESIGN. **Opposite:** THIS ORNATE, CLASSICALLY SHAPED WROUGHT-IRON GAZEBO WAS PURPOSEFULLY PLACED AWAY FROM THE HOUSE TO CREATE A TRANQUIL, SECLUDED SPOT FOR ENJOYING THE STRIKING LANDSCAPE.

LE CORBUSIER, AN INNOVATOR IN THE FIELD OF MODERN ARCHITECTURE, EXPLORED THE RELATIONSHIP OF INTERIOR AND EXTERIOR SPACES, CONSIDERING WALLS TO BE MEDIATORS BETWEEN SPACES RATHER THAN IMMUTABLE BARRIERS SEPARATING THEM. THESE OCEANSIDE DECKS, SUBTLY SEPARATED FROM THE SURROUNDING LAND AND SEA BY GLASS PANELS, CONFORM TO LE CORBUSIER'S CONCEPTUAL FRAMEWORK.

Above: ON HIS OWN REDWOOD DECK, ARCHITECT ANDY NEUMAN INSTALLED TEMPERED GLASS TO BUFFER THE PREVAILING NORTHWEST WINDS. THE GLASS SCREEN RESEMBLES A SERIES OF WINDOWS PUNCTUATING A CURVED REDWOOD WALL, AN ILLUSION THAT GIVES THE DECK A MORE ENCLOSED FEEL.

Opposite: A GLASS WINDBREAK SHELTERS BUILT-IN SEATING ON A DECK DESIGNED FOR BEACHSIDE DINING.

Opposite: ATOP A MANHATTAN BROWN-STONE, TEXTURED WHITE CANVAS DRAPED OVER A SIMPLE FRAME CREATES A CABANA-STYLE HAVEN FROM THE COMMOTION OF THE CITY BELOW. INSIDE, AN ELEGANT COPPER-FRAME LOUNGE IS STRATEGICALLY POSITIONED TO OVERLOOK THE FRAGRANT CONTAINER GARDEN. **Below:** TUCKED INTO THE CORNER OF THIS SMALL BALCONY, A SIMPLE CHAISE LOUNGE WITH CLASSICAL LINES PROVIDES A RELAXING VANTAGE POINT TO THE SURROUNDING HILLY TERRAIN.

Above: TERRACES FUNCTION AS SMALL OUTDOOR REFUGES WITHIN DENSE URBAN LIVING ENVIRONMENTS, PARTICULARLY WHEN THEY RISE ABOVE NEIGHBORING ROOFTOPS. FEATHEROCK, NATURALLY FORMED BLOCKS OF PUMICE WEIGHING EIGHTY PERCENT LESS THAN GRANITE, IS A LIGHTWEIGHT ALTERNATIVE TO BOULDERS AND A CONVINCING WAY TO BRING THE RURAL COUNTRYSIDE TO THIS CITY SKYDECK.

Left: THIS SMALL PATIO LOCATED OFF A TOWN-HOUSE IS FURNISHED MINIMALLY BUT MEMORABLY. LACY-LOOKING WHITE FURNITURE STANDS OUT AGAINST A BACKGROUND OF NATURAL COLOR, AND A WOODEN WHEELBARROW FUNCTIONS AS A PLANTER. **Below:** THIS PATIO IS SURROUNDED BY A CONCRETE-BLOCK AND WOOD STRUCTURE THAT IS SUGGESTIVE OF A HOUSE UNDER CONSTRUCTION. **Opposite:** THE IMMENSITY OF THIS OUTDOOR PATIO, PERGOLA, AND FIREPLACE—THE SLATE FLOOR TILES EACH MEASURE 24 INCHES (60CM) SQUARE—SUITS THE PROPORTIONS OF THE EXTENSIVE LAWNS AND TALL TREES BEYOND. THE PERGOLA IS WIRED FOR OUTDOOR LIGHTING

Opposite: THE OWNERS OF THIS POOL HOUSE, WHICH IS SEPARATE FROM THEIR MAIN HOUSE, WANTED AN AFTERNOON AROUND THE POOL TO FEEL LIKE A VACATION IN BERMUDA. THE BUILDING FEATURES A COPPER-AND-GLASS VAULTED SKYLIGHT THAT WARMS AND BRIGHTENS THE INTERIOR. **Above left:** THE POOL HOUSE IS COMPLETELY SELF-CONTAINED, WITH A FULLY EQUIPPED KITCHEN, STAGING AREA, AND DINING TABLE.

Above right: THE PALETTE CHOSEN FOR THE POOL HOUSE REFLECTS THE WARM, TROPICAL COLORS OF BERMUDA. THE LIGHT COLORS AND WHIMSICAL FORMS EVOKE A PLAYFUL, RELAXED ATMOSPHERE OF ESCAPE FROM EVERYDAY HUSTLE AND BUSTLE.

Left: AS THE FOCAL POINT OF BACKYARD LIVING, A POOL CAN BECOME A PERSONAL FANTASYLAND. AT THIS PRIVATE ESTATE, WATER FALLS FROM DUCTS IN THE PERGOLA, PAST NAIAD STATUES, AND INTO THE LUXURIOUS POOL. QUARTZ LAMPS HEAT THE DINING AREA, WHICH IS PARTIALLY SHADED BY AN EXTENSION OF THE PERGOLA. **Above:** THE OPEN BREEZEWAY CONNECTING OPPOSITE WINGS OF THIS HOUSE ALSO FUNCTIONS AS AN OUTDOOR DINING ROOM.

Above: THE SLIGHTLY CURVING FORM OF THIS GRAND TERRACE ECHOES ITS MOUNTAINTOP SITE, WHICH AFFORDS A 360-DEGREE VIEW OF THE VALLEY BELOW. IN KEEPING WITH THE EXPANSIVENESS OF THE LAND, LARGE COLUMNS AND AN EQUALLY GENEROUS RAILING ANCHOR THE TERRACE. **Right:** THIS RESIDENCE IN THE CALIFORNIA WINE COUNTRY, WHICH CONFORMS TO THE LOCAL TRADITION OF EXPOSED-WOOD CONSTRUCTION, POSSESSES A WHITE-PAINTED PORCH MODELED AFTER AN OLD-FASHIONED DOG TROT. THE NARROW RUN, INTEGRAL TO THE HOUSE'S TRAFFIC PATTERN, SEPARATES THE LIVING ROOM FROM THE KITCHEN. THE DECK BENEATH THE CEDAR TRUSS AFFORDS A PANORAMIC VIEW OF KNIGHTS VALLEY.

Left: THE TERRACE OF ARCHITECT JOSÉ DE YTRUBE'S HOME IN MEXICO REFLECTS REGIONAL DESIGN INFLUENCES AND OFFERS A COMFORTABLE FAMILY RETREAT. A FIREPLACE HOLLOWED OUT FROM ADOBE-COVERED MASONRY WALLS WARMS THE LAKESIDE ROOM. *EQUIPAL* CHAIRS AND STOOLS REPRESENTATIVE OF THE LOCAL STYLE OFFSET CUSHION-COVERED ADOBE BENCHES. **Above:** A RUGGED ROOFTOP TERRACE IN NORTH CAREYES HARBOR, MEXICO, COMPLEMENTS THE ROCKY HEADLAND ON WHICH THE HOUSE SITS. PASTEL WASHES SOFTEN THE PRIMITIVE-LOOKING SPACE, WHILE CUSHIONS AND A BED OF PILLOWS INVITE THE TRAVELER TO PAUSE AND EXPERIENCE THE MAJESTIC CALM OF A MEXICAN SUNSET.

PART TWO

FAMILY ROOMS

CANDACE ORD MANROE

Introduction

By virtue of its name, the family room is a lifestyle indicator. Unlike the bedroom, bathroom, kitchen, or living room, the family room points not so much to a specific, task-oriented function as to an informal, comfortable approach to living in the home that centers around family togetherness. The particular activities pursued in the family room are of less importance than the deeper value statement the room suggests: the importance of gathering, for whatever purpose, in a space designated specifically for those individuals who share the community life defined as a family.

Today, with "family values" having become a buzzword in our culture, the emphasis on home and family has never been stronger. The notion of "cocooning"—nestling into the safety and sanctuary of the home as the preferred place for spending leisure time, as opposed to seeking entertainment and diversion outside the home—emerged in the late 1980s. The momentum continues to grow, as the popularity of home entertaining and the booming home video business illustrate. Not since the 1950s have family rooms been of greater importance in planning and designing the home than they are today.

Not only does the family room in general serve as a life-style barometer for the 1990s; in its specific forms and variations, it reflects the development of other cultural phenomena in our society. This is especially true of home electronics, whose breakneck pace of technological development has left its indelible mark on the family room. To keep up, the family room must adapt and change its own form.

The family room of the 1950s had that epoch's marvel, the television, as its focal point. If the TV wasn't encased in its own cabinet as a freestanding piece of furniture, it usually rested on a TV stand or table. Of secondary importance was the hi-fi, which also was self-contained as a console model. In contrast, the family room of the 1990s is likely to have an entire home media center or even home

Opposite: Preconceived notions of the traditional den undergo radical rethinking in this space: Its fireplace and location in the back of the home make this room a den by definition, but easy stereotyping of the space stops here. The clean, contemporary room is the antithesis of the woody, rugged prototype den. From the geometric, sculpted doorway to the black-tiled ceiling, this den is a dramatic expression of its owners' sophisticated, contemporary sensibilities.

theater as its entertainment source, with components replacing casegoods and with state-of-the-art audio equipment, storage capacity for videos, CDs, and tapes, and perhaps even a movie screen for TV and video viewing, as well as a home computer.

Obviously, these changes over four decades have necessitated some revision in how the family room is designed. The '50s family room was fine for a console TV and hi-fi; it may not accommodate the accoutrements of a fully-equipped 1990s home entertainment system, which typically requires an entire wall of cabinet or shelf space. As much as any area of the home, the family room is a case of form following function.

The family room is an invention that originated in the post–World War II boom era. It was prefigured in Victorian times, when homes were commonly designed with double parlors—one for receiving guests and another for the privacy of the family. For large occasions, the two parlors could be opened up. But even in the family parlor, an abiding formality reigned, both in the architecture and the furnishings, as well as in the location of the room toward the front of the dwelling.

After World War I, families began to move to the suburbs, and the houses they built changed, becoming less formal. By World War II, this trend had become a way of life, with affordable housing transforming suburbia into the mecca of family life. The new suburban homes reflected a significantly less formal life-style characterized by backyard barbecues and neighborhood progressive suppers, in which casseroles replaced the more elegant, multi-course dinners of years gone by. This new life-style pivoted on the backyard, leading home owners to create a casual living space just off the back of the house that opened onto the yard. The traditional family room, often called a den, was the result. Not only did the room face the yard, but in another practical consideration, it was also usually adjacent to the kitchen for easy interaction between the two hubs. Another feature typical of this new room was a fireplace, which permitted the family to huddle snugly in the room, watching TV, reading, or simply communing.

In the 1970s, the family room took another turn, in some homes evolving into the "great room." This space's prototype dates back even before the Victorian era, to colonial times, when the "keeping room" was the central, most utilized space. This was the original multipurpose room, serving as both kitchen and living room, with the hearth as the focal point for cooking, staying warm, and socializing.

Like the keeping room, the great room usually incorporates a dining table and opens onto the kitchen, with no

visual barriers separating the two spaces. Unlike the early keeping room, which tended to be dark, with only a few small windows (to help keep warmth indoors), the great room often embraces impressive outdoor views through large expanses of glass, thanks to improved insulation and climate-controlled heating and cooling.

Today's family room can take at least four distinct forms, with much overlap and many variations: the traditional den, cozy with its fireplace and back-of-the-house location; the great room, larger and more open than the den, incorporating an eating table and often capturing vistas through large windows or glass doors; the recreation room, which may have traditional play equipment such as dart boards, as well as electronic entertainment, and which is frequently located in the basement; and finally, the home media center, which may be found in any room, even in a spare bedroom, that has been enlisted for this specialized service as a family room.

Whichever form the family room assumes, one theme remains constant: Of all the rooms in the home, the family room is the space that exudes warmth and a beckoning comfort. This is the place where the veil is lifted and the real personalities of the home owners are revealed. It is the room where family members gather to enjoy each other's company and it is notable for its absence of pretense, for its kick-your-shoes-off style. In the anatomy of the home, the family room is the heart.

Above: A COMMONSENSE APPROACH TO DESIGNING THE DEN IS TO GO WITH THE HOME'S PERVADING ARCHITECTURAL STYLE. IN THIS CASE, THE ARCHITECTURE IS REGIONAL, CELEBRATING A SOUTHWESTERN INFLUENCE. THE DEN INCORPORATES THAT STYLE'S CHARACTERISTIC JUXTAPOSITION OF RUGGED BEAMS AND CLEAN, WHITE WALLS; OF DECORATIVE TILES AT THE FIREPLACE AND SPARE ACCESSORIES (SUCH AS THE COW SKULL ABOVE); AND OF COMFORT ARTICULATED IN A CONTEMPORARY LEXICON.

THE TRADITIONAL DEN

Moving from public spaces of the home to the den, you notice the change immediately. The furnishings are more inviting and less precious; sofas and chairs are deeper, softer, and dressed in upholsteries that invite you to curl up in them. The walls change from smooth paper, drywall, or formal plaster to textured paneling or rough-hewn boards. Even the flooring is different, whether harder or softer, having an easy-to-clean, low-maintenance factor distinguishable from floors in the remainder of the home.

This is the traditional den, the original family room popularized after World War II. Generally situated in the rear of the home and adjoining the kitchen, it is the informal living space devoted to the family. Here, snacks can be nibbled without a fuss; TV, videos, and stereo can be enjoyed without worries about hiding electronics gadgetry; toddlers and pets, as a rule, can wander at ease.

In its post–World War II form, the den suggested a retreat, a place for hibernation, darker than the other living spaces of the home. Deep-stained paneling and a brick or stone fireplace were *de rigueur*, as was an overall somber palette. Today's den can still possess this dark, enveloping quality, but its definition has broadened considerably. The den in the '90s might be filled with soft lights from a bank of windows and feature whitewashed cedar paneling, a pickled oak floor, and an inviting, white-painted fireplace. The hatches no longer have to be battened; doors or windows can be flung open to the outdoors, creating a cheery, inviting effect.

Today's den may be a protected haven, an open, relaxed gathering place, or any variation thereof; what every den has in common is the feeling of home.

Opposite: THE BEST OF BOTH WORLDS, THIS TRADITIONAL FAMILY ROOM OFFERS THE ENVELOPING COMFORT OF THE QUINTESSENTIAL DEN, WITH ITS STONE FIREPLACE AND SOFT FURNISHINGS, AS WELL AS AN AIRIER, MORE CONTEMPORARY SENSE OF LIGHT AND SPACE, THANKS TO THE MULTITUDE OF WINDOWS, PALE PALETTE, AND HIGH CEILING.

Left: IN A LOG HOME, THE INVITING FAMILY ROOM IS A NATURAL EXTENSION OF AN ABUNDANCE OF EXISTING BUILDING MATERIALS, REQUIRING LITTLE MORE THAN TAKING ADVANTAGE OF WHAT THE HOME INHERENTLY HAS TO OFFER. CHINKED WIDE-PINE LOG WALLS AND A PALER PINE FLOOR CREATE A LODGE-LIKE WARMTH, COMPLEMENTED BY A TOWERING FIELDSTONE FIREPLACE. BOOKSHELVES, GAMEBOARDS, COMFORTABLE SEATING, AND A MIX OF ANTIQUES AND NEW FURNISHINGS ARE THE FINISHING TOUCHES.

Right: THE LONG, LEAN LINES OF A LOGGIA CREATE AN IDEAL SPACE FOR A DEN, WITH BREEZY ACCESS TO THE OUTDOORS. THIS RESTFUL ROOM FEATURES AN ECLECTIC MIX OF TRADITIONAL YET COMFORTABLE SEATING WITH CONTEMPORARY ART AND ACCESSORIES, CAPTURING THE VARIED INTERESTS OF THE OWNERS.

Above: ONE OF THE APPEALING QUALITIES OF THE TRADITIONAL DEN TODAY IS ITS ABILITY TO REFLECT THE DECORATING STYLE OF THE OWNERS. DARK-PANELED WALLS AND BRAIDED RUGS AREN'T FOR EVERYONE, AS THIS MORE DRESSED-UP DEN ILLUSTRATES. HERE, TASTE TAKES A FORMAL TURN, WITH PERSONALITY FINDING EXPRESSION IN A COLLECTION OF ANTIQUE BLUE-AND-WHITE PORCELAIN AND PERIOD ANTIQUES. STILL, COMFORT IS THE KEY TO THE SPACE, WITH WINGBACK CHAIRS PROVIDING SOFT SPOTS FOR COZYING UP WITH A BOOK OR SIMPLY ENJOYING A FIRE.

Left: IN SOME HOMES, THE ONLY DISTINCTION BETWEEN A LIVING ROOM AND A FAMILY ROOM LIES IN THE LEVEL OF INFORMALITY AND BECKONING LIVABILITY OF THE SPACE. ANY DOUBTS ABOUT WHICH FUNCTION THIS ROOM SERVES ARE REMOVED BY THE INVITING MISSION ROCKING CHAIR AND THE INFORMAL PLACEMENT OF OTHER SEATED PIECES.

Right: EVEN A CALIFORNIA HOME IN THE CANYONS OF LOS ANGELES HAS A WARM HEART AT ITS CENTER, IN THE FORM OF A COZY FAMILY ROOM REPLETE WITH PANELED WALLS, ECLECTIC FABRICS, AND A MENAGERIE OF FAVORITE ANIMAL-THEMED ACCESSORIES. THIS SPACE LEAVES LITTLE DOUBT AS TO THE SINGULAR TASTES OF ITS OWNERS.

Above: Designed to serve the family, not to alienate it, this den incorporates an interplay of light and dark for a mood that's at once uplifting and soothing. In a surprising departure from the quintessential den, the paneling is not dark, but rather a source of light, painted a pale, creamy hue. The warmer tones emanate from the fireplace brick and the burnished palette of the upholstery. Flea-market finds give clues to the family's interests.

Above: MORE THAN ANY OTHER SPACE IN THE HOME, THE FAMILY ROOM ALLOWS THE REAL PERSONALITIES OF THE OWNERS TO SPEAK WITHOUT RESERVATION. THE OWNERS OF THIS HOME HAVE AN UNERRING EYE FOR DESIGN THAT ENABLES ELOQUENT EXPRESSION OF A RANGE OF INTERESTS, FROM CONTEMPORARY FURNISHINGS LIKE THE UNDULATING COCKTAIL TABLE AND CHROME-AND-LEATHER SEATING TO FOLK ART, LITERATURE, AND THE OCCASIONAL FUNKY FIND, CREATING A TRULY PERSONAL VERSION OF THE TRADITIONAL DEN.

Above: A CENTRAL FUNCTION OF THE DEN IS TO SOOTHE. THE IDEA OF THE DEN AS

A TRANQUIL HAVEN FOR ENJOYING MORE REFLECTIVE MOMENTS IS BEAUTIFULLY CONVEYED IN

THIS SERENE ROOM, IN WHICH THE WALLS, CEILING, FIREPLACE, AND FURNISHINGS

ARE SO CLOSELY RELATED IN COLOR VALUE AS TO GIVE A MONOCHROMATIC IMPRESSION.

THE WOVEN NAVAJO RUG, THE ONLY PATTERN IN THE ROOM, PRECLUDES THE POSSIBILITY OF

ANY RESIDUAL CHILL FROM THE SUBTLE PALETTE.

Opposite: A RICH, MASCULINE FLAVOR PERVADES THIS DEN, FROM THE PICTURE-FRAME PANELING AND BUILT-IN BOOK-SHELVES TO THE VIBRANT RED LEATHER WINGBACK CHAIRS AND DEEP BLUE CURTAINS WITH RED TRIM. A SOFT THROW PILED ON THE ARM OF A CHAIR, A PLATE OF APPLES, AND A GAME OF DOMINOES PROVE THAT THE DEN, NO MATTER HOW REFINED, IS USER-FRIENDLY FOR THE ENTIRE FAMILY. **Above:** AS THE TRUEST MIRROR OF THE HOMEOWNER'S SELF, THE FAMILY ROOM IN THIS HOME POINTS TO A PERSONALITY THAT IS DEFINITELY MARCHING TO A DIFFERENT DRUM, WITH AN APPRECIATION FOR THE OFFBEAT AND THE UNEXPECTED. THE COMBINATIONS HERE ARE JOLTING——MASSIVE ARCHITECTURAL FEATURES TOWER OVER TINY TABLES; STYLES RANGE FROM TURN-OF-THE-CENTURY ARCHITECTURE TO 1960S FURNISHINGS.

Below: THIS ROOM TAKES MAXIMUM ADVANTAGE OF THE TRADITIONAL LOCATION OF THE DEN AT THE REAR OF THE HOME. THE ENTIRE EXTERIOR WALL HAS BEEN OPENED UP WITH AN EXPANSE OF CUSTOM WINDOWS HIGH IN STYLE AND DIMENSION, ALLOWING THE ROOM TO EXTEND ONTO A DECK OVERLOOKING THE BACKYARD.

Above: WARM PLAID UPHOLSTERY FABRICS, A WOVEN INDIAN RUG, AND OTHER SOUTHWESTERN TEXTILES CREATE A VIBRANT ATMOSPHERE THAT'S CASUAL ENOUGH FOR FAMILY USE, YET SUFFICIENTLY STYLISH FOR ENTERTAINING GUESTS. THIS FAMILY ROOM EMBRACES THE CONCEPT OF THE TRADITIONAL DEN WITH ITS OLD-FASHIONED IRON STOVE, AND ENLARGES IT WITH ITS SOARING, TRUSSED PINE CEILING.

Above: A DEN IN THE HEART OF THE CITY DRAWS ITS CHARACTER FROM ITS URBAN ENVIRONS, ACHIEVING A COOL, SOPHISTICATED ELEGANCE. WISELY, THE OWNERS TURNED THE CITYSCAPE JUST OUTSIDE INTO AN INTEGRAL PART OF THE ROOM BY EMBRACING THE VIEW WITH WINDOWS LEFT COVERED ONLY BY A SHEER VALANCE, RATHER THAN CAMOUFLAGED BY A DISGUISE OF HEAVY DRAPERY.

Below: A FONDNESS FOR FOLK ART, ESPECIALLY WITH A HISPANIC FLAVOR, IS CLEARLY ANNOUNCED IN THIS SMALL DEN. MUCH OF THE ROOM'S APPEAL DERIVES FROM THE UNEXPECTED MIX OF TRADITIONAL ARCHITECTURE WITH FOLKSY FURNISHINGS.

Above: A PAIR OF DUTCH-STYLE DOORS THAT SLIDE ON A ROD, RATHER THAN OPEN AT THE HINGE, ARE THE FIRST CLUE TO THE UNUSUAL IN THIS FAMILY ROOM. DECORATIVE PAINT TREATMENTS IN A PALE GOLDEN HUE ADORN WALLS AND CEILING, SUGGESTING A PLAYFUL AMBIENCE, BUT THE FURNISHINGS THEMSELVES ARE DARK AND LEATHER, MORE TYPICAL OF THE CLASSIC DEN. THE EFFECT IS INTERESTING AND PERSONAL, DEFYING AN EASY CLASSIFICATION OF DECORATING STYLE. **Opposite:** DRAMATIC SHEER AUBERGINE CURTAINS ACCENTUATING THE HIGH-FLUNG TRADITIONAL ARCHITECTURE OF THIS SPACE MIGHT SIGNAL A FORMAL LIVING ROOM, RATHER THAN A FAMILY ROOM WHOSE PURPOSE IS LIFE-STYLE MORE THAN "LOOK." BUT THERE IS NO MISTAKING THIS SPACE'S DESIGNATION AS A DEN, THANKS TO THE CASUAL PLACEMENT OF FURNITURE, THE INCLUSION OF A WELL-WORN FAVORITE FAMILY CHAIR, AND THE DESIGN'S ORIENTATION AROUND THE FIREPLACE.

Below: THE IDEA THAT A DEN MUST BE A SMALL, COMPACT SPACE WITH A DARK, ENVELOPING ATMOSPHERE IS REFUTED BY THIS SPACIOUS FAMILY ROOM, IN WHICH TRUSSED CEILINGS DECLARE LOFTY SPACE OVERHEAD AND THE WHITE AND GLASS WALLS CELEBRATE AIRY OPENNESS. THERE IS NO DANGER OF THE ROOM FEELING STARK OR STERILE, HOWEVER, WITH ITS STONE FIREPLACE, RUGGED WOOD FLOORING, AND CASUAL FURNISHINGS.

Above: THE KIVA FIREPLACE AND PLASTER WALLS IN THIS ADOBE HOME PROVIDE THE DECORATIVE ORIENTATION OF THE FAMILY ROOM. WALLS ARE LEFT UNADORNED, MAKING TEXTURAL STATEMENTS IN THEMSELVES, AND WRAPAROUND MODULAR SOFA SEATING SNUGGLES UP TO THE FIREPLACE, WITH ONLY A SMALL COCKTAIL TABLE IN THE CENTER BY WAY OF ADDITIONAL FURNISHINGS.

Opposite: A TRUMPETBLAST OF COLOR AND MODERN ART BRINGS LIFE TO THE ELEGANT ARCHITECTURE OF THIS TRADITIONAL DEN, SOFTENING WHAT COULD HAVE BEEN AN INTIMIDATING ENVIRONMENT. ALTHOUGH THE ROOM EXUDES PEDIGREE, NOT ONLY FROM ITS RICHLY DETAILED PANELING BUT ALSO DUE TO THE CALIBER OF ITS CONTEMPORARY ART AND FURNISHINGS, IT NONETHELESS HAS ALL THE INVITING ALLURE OF A CLASSIC DEN: SEATING IS CAPACIOUS AND COMFORTABLE, WELL PLACED FOR THE ENJOYMENT OF CONVERSATION AND A CRACKLING FIRE.

Below: WITH THE FIREPLACE AS ITS FOCAL POINT, THIS DEN ENSURES ENJOYMENT OF THE HEARTH WITH A FURNITURE ARRANGEMENT THAT POSITIONS A PAIR OF COMFORTABLE WINGBACK CHAIRS AT FIRESIDE, WITH A FUNCTIONAL TABLE IN BETWEEN. CHAIR FABRICS ARE IN THE SAME COLOR FAMILY BUT IN TWO DISTINCTIVE PATTERNS, ENHANCING THE FEELING OF UNSTUDIED STYLE.

Above: AN ANTIQUE HOME PRESENTS A UNIQUE OPPORTUNITY FOR DESIGNING A FAMILY ROOM THAT BESPEAKS A HOMEY, PERSONAL CHARM. THE ORIGINAL HEADBOARD CEILING, ALONG WITH EXPOSED HEWN BEAMS, WAS RETAINED IN THIS SPACE TO CREATE AMBIENCE OVERHEAD, WITH A HANGING DISPLAY OF DRIED HERBS AND ANTIQUE BASKETS. A BRAIDED RUG, YESTERYEAR FABRIC PATTERNS, FOLK ART, AND ANTIQUE ACCESSORIES AND FURNISHINGS REINFORCE THE OLD-STYLE WARMTH OF THE ARCHITECTURE WHILE AT THE SAME TIME EXPRESSING THE FAMILY'S INTERESTS.

Above: Despite its relatively small space, this den projects warmth and a singular robust flair due, in large part, to the selection of red as the dominant color. Repeated on furniture coverings, other textiles, and a vibrant lamp shade, the bold red hue draws the room together, surprisingly enhancing rather than reducing its sense of spaciousness.

Opposite: THIS CLASSIC DEN, WITH ITS DARK PANELED WALLS AND FIREPLACE, ESCHEWS A DATED LOOK BY INCORPORATING FURNISHINGS THAT ARTICULATE COLOR BLOCKS—ONE OF DECORATING'S NEWEST LOOKS.

Above: IN A CONTEMPORARY HOME, THE FAMILY ROOM DOESN'T HAVE TO BE AN AFTERTHOUGHT, A TACKED-ON HOMAGE TO TRADITIONAL DESIGN. INSTEAD, AS EVIDENCED BY THIS SPACE, IT CAN BE AN INHERENT PART OF THE ARCHITECTURE. BUILT-IN BANQUETTE SEATING CIRCUMSCRIBES THE FIREPLACE, WHILE THE DEN ITSELF IS SUNKEN, DESCENDING FROM A SMALL ATRIUM—ALL PART OF THE ORIGINAL ARCHITECTURAL DESIGN.

Above: As one of the most personal spaces in the home, the family room presents an opportunity to engage in wish-fulfillment. This home's ranch-style architecture is a launching pad for realizing the Wild West fantasy. The western theme pervades the space through bronzes, covered-wagon accessories and art, wagon-wheel furniture, and Indian rugs.

Left: THE SERENE, SETTLED AMBIENCE OF A GRACIOUS LIBRARY OR STUDY CHARACTERIZES THIS DEN. BOOKS LINE THE WALLS FOR LAZY PERUSAL, WHILE A WET BAR FACILITATES A DIFFERENT SORT OF AFTER-DINNER RELAXATION. ENJOYMENT OF THE BLAZING FIRE IS ENCOURAGED BY THE PRESENCE OF PLUSH CHAIRS AND A PLUMP SOFA.

Right: BEAUTIFULLY BALANCED WITH ITS SYMMETRICALLY PLACED WINDOWS AND FURNISHINGS, THIS DEN IS THE BEST OF BOTH WORLDS: LIGHT AND AIRY, YET AT THE SAME TIME COZY AND COMFORTING. THE DESIGN IS INFORMAL YET TRADITIONAL, WITH SUBTLE OVERTONES OF COUNTRY.

The Great Room

With its open spaces that serve a multitude of needs, the great room caters to the way families live today. Like the colonial era's keeping room, the great room often features a fireplace and seating area, plus a dining table, accommodating the functions of everyday living and eating, which so often overlap. This room not only serves the needs of the family, but is also an ideal space for entertaining. Cozy seating areas facilitate conversations, while a dining table placed in the same room means that hors d'oeuvres may be enjoyed without having to move from room to room. The wide walls of the great room afford ample space for freestanding entertainment units or built-in shelving to house home electronics equipment. With its multipurpose functions, the great room promises to be the most lived-in space in the modern home.

The great room lends itself to almost any architectural style, from early primitive to contemporary high-tech. Typically, the ceiling of the great room is lofty, enhancing the already capacious sense of space. In a rustic, country-style home, the great room's ceiling might feature old salvaged hand-hewn beams that are left exposed for rugged, vintage interest. In a contemporary home, the ceiling of the great room might be vaulted and painted a pristine white, emphasizing spare lines and form more than texture or ornamentation.

Like the den, the great room is usually situated at the rear of the house, either opening onto or facing the grounds behind the home. It is not uncommon for the room to capitalize on its large scale by embracing panoramic views through broad expanses of glass. Such wide, high windows make the room one of the brightest and lightest in the house, in contrast to the traditional den, which tends to be a bit more enclosed and enveloping.

No matter whether it is furnished in a spare, streamlined fashion or a cozy, old-fashioned country style, the great room is perfect for the modern family life-style.

Opposite: As lifestyles change, the function of the family room changes, too. In many homes, a great room, which has more space to house electronic entertainment equipment, is the preferred choice over the smaller, traditional den. Here, the brick fireplace incorporates an electronics niche.

Above: A STEP-UP KITCHEN OPENS ONTO THIS SUNKEN FAMILY ROOM, CREATING

A CASUAL ATMOSPHERE WITH A CONVENIENT, PRACTICAL FUNCTION: THE HOST OR HOSTESS

NEED NOT DISAPPEAR INTO THE KITCHEN FOR FINAL MEAL PREPARATIONS, BUT CAN EASILY

COMMUNE WITH GUESTS OR FAMILY MEMBERS SEATED JUST BELOW.

Left: THE GREAT ROOM, ONE OF THE MOST POPULAR FORMS OF FAMILY ROOM IN TODAY'S HOMES, IS BY DEFINITION OPEN AND SPACIOUS. IN THIS HOME, PERIOD ARCHITECTURE AND COUNTRY STYLE COMBINE WITH A MODERN SENSIBILITY—ONLY A COUNTER WORK SPACE DIVIDES THE KITCHEN FROM THE LARGER EXPANSE OF FAMILY ROOM—AND EVEN THE COUNTER IS OPEN AT THE TOP, SANS CUPBOARDS.

Right: THIS GREAT ROOM DIVIDES ITS FUNCTIONS INTO TWO DISTINCT AREAS: A SNUG SPACE FOR READING OR VISITING WITH FAMILY AND FRIENDS ON COMFORTABLE CHAIRS AND SOFAS, AND A SMALL DINING AREA FOR TAKING AN INFORMAL MEAL OR A CUP OF COFFEE. THE KITCHEN OPENS ONTO THE DINING AREA, ALLOWING FAMILY MEMBERS TO MOVE EASILY FROM COOKING TO DINING TO SOCIALIZING.

Above: THIS GREAT ROOM COMBINES DIVERSE FEATURES TO CUSTOM-FIT ITS OWNERS. THE LOW-SLUNG ARCHITECTURE WITH ITS RECESSED LIGHTING AND EXPANSES OF GLASS IS CONTEMPORARY, WHILE THE FIREPLACE MANTEL IS TRADITIONAL. ANTIQUES ADD A RUGGED PRESENCE TO THE CLEAN, NEUTRAL PALETTE.

Above: DECKED IN SLICK WHITE, WITH LINEAR CONTEMPORARY WINDOWS, SKYLIGHTS, AND HIGH-TECH BLACK ACCENTS, THIS FAMILY ROOM PUTS A FRESH SPIN ON THE IDEA OF COZY. THE MODULAR SEATING IS COMFORTABLE AND BECKONING, INVITING FAMILY MEMBERS AND FRIENDS TO RELAX BEFORE THE FIRE. INTERESTINGLY, THIS SPACE IS DEVOID OF ANY OF THE BRIC-A-BRAC OR HOMEY ACCESSORIES THAT TYPICALLY CHARACTERIZE A FAMILY ROOM, WITH THE RESULT THAT FAMILY MEMBERS ARE ENCOURAGED TO CONCENTRATE ON EACH OTHER.

Above: More than the public spaces in the home, the family room represents an opportunity to reveal the unique personalities and predilections of the home owners. This great room has a high-style design that reflects the one-of-a-kind aesthetic tastes of its owners. The elephant-patterned batik fabric on the sofa and above the doorway combine with the zebra-striped rug in the dining alcove to impart an ethnic flavor to the room, while favorite objets d'art displayed on vertical shelving add a personal touch.

Below: THIS CONTEMPORARY BEACHFRONT GREAT ROOM COMBINES PERIOD FURNITURE, COLLECTIBLES, AND ART FOR A SUNNY UPDATE OF THE EIGHTEENTH-CENTURY KEEPING ROOM.

Above: ANY NOTIONS THAT A FAMILY ROOM AND STELLAR STYLE ARE MUTUALLY EXCLUSIVE TERMS STOPS HERE. THE GRAND, CONTEMPORARY ARCHITECTURE OF THIS GREAT ROOM, WITH ITS SOARING CEILINGS AND BOLD GEOMETRY, MAKES A FAMILY GATHERING AN AESTHETIC EXPERIENCE OF THE HIGHEST ORDER.

Above: THE GREAT ROOM DOESN'T HAVE TO ENCOMPASS AN ENORMOUS AREA TO GET THE JOB DONE. ALL THE NECESSARY INGREDIENTS—A FIREPLACE, COMFORTABLE SEATING, AND A DINING TABLE—ARE PRESENT IN THIS MODERATELY SIZED SPACE.

Left: A CHEF'S DREAM, THIS GREAT ROOM ALLOWS CULINARY DUTIES TO BE PERFORMED WITHOUT A PAUSE IN CONVERSATION. THE KITCHEN WORK COUNTER (VISIBLE IN THE FOREFRONT OF THE PHOTO) OVERLOOKS THE FAMILY ROOM'S DINING SPACE AND SEATING AREA, PROVING THE MERITS OF A MULTIFUNCTIONAL ROOM DESIGN.

Right: AN INFORMAL, INDIGENOUS ARCHITECTURAL STYLE REMINISCENT OF THE WORK OF FRANK LLOYD WRIGHT CREATES AN APPROPRIATELY WARM ATMOSPHERE FOR A GREAT ROOM. THE DINING CHAIRS AND WOOD FLOORING COMPLEMENT THE ARCHITECTURE, CREATING AN INVITING SPACE THAT ISN'T RELIANT ON ADDITIONAL DECORATIVE OBJECTS FOR ITS COMPELLING AMBIENCE.

Above: TAKING AN L-SHAPE FROM THE OUTLINE OF THE KITCHEN,

THIS GREAT ROOM PROVIDES TWO DISCRETE AREAS—ONE FOR CONVERSATION IN FRONT

OF THE FIREPLACE, ANOTHER FOR CASUAL DINING IN FRONT OF THE WINDOWS, WITH NO

VISUAL BARRIERS IN BETWEEN. THE CURVACEOUS SHAPES AND DEEP COLORS IN THE SEATING

AREA MAKE IT A WARM AND INVITING CORNER.

Above: A family room can be created from virtually any existing space in the home. Here, a solarium serves the function of a great room, complete with an intimate seating area before the fireplace, electronic entertainment equipment stored in a console, and a casual dining area. With the glass walls and ceiling, the room is as airy as the outdoors itself.

Right: Saturated in jewel-tone colors and funky cowboy charm, this great room is where the Old West meets creature comforts head-on, with some lively, fun results. **Below:** Despite its streamlined contemporary style, this family room has its origins in colonial times, in the keeping room that incorporated a seating area for family within close proximity to the kitchen fireplace. No fireplace graces this room, but its open flow into the kitchen nonetheless echoes the idea of the erstwhile keeping room.

Just for Fun

Among the types of family rooms, the media rooms and play or recreation rooms offer the greatest flexibility in terms of architecture and location within the home. Almost any room in the house, including a spare guest room or an open room in the basement, can suffice. Rather than operating as a general-purpose hangout, this family room is geared specifically to entertainment.

As a media room (or TV room, as it was known before home electronics became increasingly sophisticated, affordable, and available), all the space really needs is adequate room for setting up equipment and providing comfortable seating. This makes the media room an attractive option as a family room in a home whose floor plan includes only one living space: A bedroom, study, unused garage, or any other spare space, regardless of its architectural interest (or lack thereof), may be easily converted to serve this purpose. A fireplace is a luxury, not a staple, as are a view and space for a dining table. It makes no difference whether the media room opens into the kitchen or onto the backyard. No wonder many families find the media room a convenient solution for freeing up a single living room from potentially space-stealing and visually obtrusive TV and stereo equipment.

Similarly, the play or recreation room has no etched-in-stone standards of form. In regions of the country in which houses include basements, the play room often is relegated to this lower level. And for practical reasons: The basement serves as a noise shield for the remainder of the home, and it can have a lower-maintenance, less-finished appearance that better suits the play function. Parents appreciate the virtues of a rec room designated especially for children: Toys, noise, and playmates can be indulged freely, without disrupting the more organized life-style of the adults. Of course, the rec room can also serve as a playground for adults. Pool tables, dart boards, game tables, TVs, stereos, and displays of sporting equipment find a comfortable home here, which might be awkward or impossible in more integrated living spaces of the home.

Opposite: One form of family room hinges on the philosophy of sheer fun. This exuberant space comes to life with a colorful collection of 1950s and '60s toys, furniture, buttons, and other collectibles. The fun television, guitar, and map fit snugly into a design that happily pleads a case for play.

Right: A MORE REFINED FAMILY ROOM DEVOTED TO PLAY AND OTHER PERSONAL PURSUITS HAS A CLEAN, NO-CLUTTER LOOK WITH SNOW-WHITE WALLS AND FURNISHINGS. BUT WITH A GAME TABLE AT ITS CENTER AND BUILT-IN BOOKSHELVES AT ITS FLANKS, THE ROOM CLEARLY IS DESIGNED WITH FUNCTION IN MIND. **Below:** A HIGH-GLOSS MEDIA ROOM THAT IS A SALIENT STATEMENT OF CONTEMPORARY DESIGN IS AN APPROPRIATE BACKDROP FOR THE SOPHISTICATED ELECTRONIC ENTERTAINMENT EQUIPMENT IT HOUSES. BLACK LACQUERED SHELVING HOLDS A COLLECTION OF PERIOD ENTERTAINMENT COLLECTIBLES, PROVIDING AN IRONIC COUNTERPOINT TO THE ROOM'S STATE-OF-THE-ART, HIGH-TECH FEEL.

Opposite: IN A DEPARTURE FROM THE TYPICAL FAMILY REC ROOM, WHICH OFTEN FEATURES CUSHIONY FURNITURE THAT INVITES SPRAWLING UPON, THIS GRAPHIC SPACE, WITH ITS SQUARE MOTIFS IN WOOD, HOSTS COLORFUL CHAIRS, BARSTOOLS, AND A TABLE AS THE MOST FUNCTIONAL MEANS TO AN END. THE TABLE AND BAR CAN SERVE AS SURFACES FOR INFORMAL MEALS OR GAMES, WHILE THE CHAIRS PROVIDE SEATS AS VANTAGE POINTS FOR WATCHING TELEVISION, FOR CONVERSATION, OR FOR READING.

Above: STRICTLY FOR KIDS, THIS FAMILY PLAY ROOM IS EVERY CHILD'S FANTASY. WITH HOT-AIR

BALLOONS SOARING ACROSS THE WALLS AND PRIMARY-COLORED BANQUETTE SEATING,

THE MULTIFARIOUS SPACE IS A STIMULATING ENVIRONMENT FOR DEVELOPMENT THROUGH PLAY.

Left: THIS FAMILY ROOM IN THE CITY IS A COMPATIBLE EXTENSION OF THE VIEWS IT EMBRACES THROUGH LARGE, PLATE-GLASS WINDOWS. QUIETLY SOPHISTICATED WITH A NO-PATTERN, NEUTRAL PALETTE THAT INCLUDES A SMATTERING OF CHIC BLACK LEATHER, IT IS AN ABOVE-IT-ALL RETREAT FOR WATCHING TELEVISION OR ENJOYING A DRINK FROM ITS HIGH-RISE VANTAGE POINT.

Right: THIS RECREATION ROOM EMBRACES THE CAREFREE JOYS OF CHILDHOOD WITH A BOLDLY COLORED DESIGN AND LOFTY CONTEMPORARY ARCHITECTURE ANY ADULT CAN APPRECIATE. THE RED AND YELLOW PALETTE ESTABLISHED IN THE FURNISHINGS EXTENDS TO THE ARCHITECTURE, AS SEEN IN THE BRILLIANT, DIAGONAL STRIPES ON A FREESTANDING ARCHITECTURAL ARMOIRE AND THE WOOD TRIM AND ROLL-UP SHADES ON THE WINDOWS.

Above: FURNITURE MANUFACTURERS HAVE RALLIED TO THE MARKET DEMAND FOR QUALITY CASEGOODS TO HOUSE SOPHISTICATED MEDIA-ROOM ELECTRONICS. ALL OF THE FAMILY'S HOME ENTERTAINMENT EQUIPMENT CAN BE HOUSED IN THIS SINGLE PIECE, FACILITATING THE UNCLUTTERED DESIGN THAT CHARACTERIZES THE SPARE YET COZY FAMILY ROOM.

Above: WITH ADEQUATE PLANNING AND A LITTLE INGENUITY, BEAUTIFUL TRADITIONAL ARCHITECTURE CAN PLAY HOST TO HOME ELECTRONICS IN A FAMILY ROOM THAT PROVES MODERN-DAY PASTIMES CAN PEACEFULLY COEXIST WITH THE MOST GRACEFUL OF INTERIORS.

Above: PLANNING IS THE KEY TO THE SUCCESS OF THIS ELEGANT, DELICIOUSLY SIMPLE CONTEMPORARY
FAMILY ROOM THAT SERVES THE OWNERS' HOME-MEDIA NEEDS. STRIPPED OF SUPERFLUOUS HARDWARE,
A WALL OF BUILT-IN SHELVING AND CABINETRY THAT ALSO HOUSES A LARGE-SCREEN TELEVISION, STEREO
COMPONENTS, AND A BAR GIVES THE SPACE ITS STREAMLINED LOOK.

Above: HIGH TECH'S COLD EDGE MELTS AWAY IN THIS WARM FAMILY ROOM, THANKS TO THE TERRA-COTTA TILE FLOOR,

BECKONING SEATING, AND THE FAMILY'S READING MATERIALS AND TROPHIES ON A WALL OF BUILT-IN BOOKSHELVES.

STILL, THE AUDIO EQUIPMENT THAT IS HOUSED IN A FLOOR-TO-CEILING CUSTOM WALL UNIT IS STATE OF-THE-ART.

Below: HOME ELECTRONICS ARE AN INSTITUTION OF TODAY'S FAMILY LIFE AND, THEREFORE, A PRIMARY FEATURE OF TODAY'S FAMILY ROOMS. THIS SOPHISTICATED DEN TAKES THE CHILL OFF ELECTRONICS EQUIPMENT BY CONTAINING IT WITHIN A WARM WOOD ANTIQUE ARMOIRE. WHEN NOT ACTIVELY ENGAGED, THE TELEVISION CAN DISAPPEAR BEHIND CLOSED DOORS.

Above: EVEN IF THE FAMILY'S ENTERTAINMENT NEEDS ARE IN CONFLICT WITH THEIR DECORATING GOALS, WITH A LITTLE CREATIVITY, A HAPPY SOLUTION CAN STILL BE ATTAINED. HERE, THE SOFT WHITE THEME OF THE FAMILY ROOM REIGNS SUPREME, AS A RESULT OF WHITE FOLDING DOORS THAT, WHEN CLOSED, GIVE THE ROOM A UNIFIED, SERENE LOOK, YET WHEN OPEN, ALLOW THE TELEVISION AND BAR TO BE ENJOYED.

Above: WHEN THE TELEVISION AND STEREO ARE FREQUENTLY EMPLOYED, IT MAKES PERFECT SENSE TO INTEGRATE THEM INTO THE DESIGN OF THE FAMILY ROOM. IN THIS GRACEFUL SPACE, THE UTILITARIAN ELECTRONICS BLEND INTO THE DECOR AS PART OF BUILT-IN SHELVING THAT ALSO DISPLAYS BOOKS AND COLLECTIBLES.

Above: EVEN IF SPACE IS AT A PREMIUM, THE FAMILY ROOM CAN SERVE A MULTITUDE OF FUNCTIONS IF INNOVATIVELY DESIGNED. A TELEVISION AND STEREO EQUIPMENT OCCUPY MINIMAL SPACE AND PRESENT MINIMAL VISUAL OBSTRUCTION IN THIS SMALL FAMILY ROOM AS A RESULT OF A NARROW STRIP OF BUILT-IN SHELVING THAT EXTENDS ALMOST TO THE CEILING. THE ROOM RETAINS A SYMMETRICAL BALANCE BECAUSE THE SHELVING'S HEIGHT, WIDTH, AND MOLDING IDENTICALLY MATCH THAT OF THE DOOR ON THE OPPOSITE SIDE OF THE FIREPLACE. **Opposite:** KNOTTY-PINE WALLS AND CEILING AND A STRATEGICALLY PLACED SKYLIGHT LEND A LODGE LOOK TO THIS REC ROOM. THE POOL TABLE IS THE FOCAL POINT, BUT BANQUETTE SEATING AROUND THE ROOM'S PERIMETER ALLOWS FOR LOUNGING WITH A BOOK OR JUST PASSING TIME. A SPORTS THEME IS ARTICULATED WITH WALL ART, WHICH INCLUDES FAMILY SPORTS PHOTOS, AWARDS, AND TROPHIES.

Personal Profile

In all its variations, the family room reflects the interior portrait—the true self—of the family that occupies it. The impersonal facade of the home's public spaces stops here. Family rooms express the identity and interests of the family through collectibles that the family truly loves—objects that tell more than show; through family photos that might clutter or disrupt the design of a more formal living space; through family heirlooms such as a grandmother's wedding dress, shadow-boxed and hung on the wall; or through musical instruments and favorite books—including paperbacks, not just coffee-table curiosities.

The family room isn't about impressing but rather, expressing. As the heart of the home, the family room has an obligation to project a sense of safety, security, and comfort. Its first call to duty is to be entirely livable. There's no room for anything too precious here. Comfortable seating is essential—big, overstuffed sectionals, sofas, and chairs; recliners; and rocking chairs that really work. Patterns and textures should invite use, rather than prohibit it. Nothing is too fussy or incompatible with wear or spills.

For all its comfort and low maintenance, the family room is anything but dull. In the home's interior design, this room can be the most audacious, featuring brighter colors than are found in more formal spaces. It even can be designed in a totally different style—such as cowboy or lodge—that would be inappropriate for the entire home. It is rich in textural interest, from rough, pickled cedar siding to ripply Saltillo tiles or lumpy wool Berber carpeting.

The family room is about how you live, but it's also about who you are.

Opposite: A SENSE OF YESTERYEAR ADDS HOMEY COMFORT TO THIS FAMILY ROOM THROUGH ANTIQUE ROCKING HORSES AND OTHER OLD COLLECTIBLES. THE WHITE UPHOLSTERY FABRICS AND TABLE SKIRT PREVENT THE SPACE FROM BECOMING BUSY, SERVING AS "AIR" AGAINST THE RICH, PATTERNED RUG. **Above:** FURNITURE ARRANGEMENT BISECTS THIS FAMILY ROOM INTO A LIBRARY AREA AND A CONVERSATION AREA, WITHOUT THE AID OF ARCHITECTURE.

Left: ONE FAMILY'S DESIRE TO BRING RUSTIC, OUTDOOR WARMTH TO THE PLAIN WHITE ARCHITECTURE OF ITS FAMILY ROOM IS BEAUTIFULLY EXECUTED IN THIS SMALL SPACE, WITH ITS RICH TEXTURE, COLOR, AND "FOUND" ACCESSORIES. ADDING ARCHITECTURE WHERE THERE IS NONE IS A ROW OF TALL TWIG BRANCHES RISING UP BEHIND THE SOFA. RATTAN AND IRON FURNISHINGS, A TWIG BASKET, A WOVEN FISHING CREEL, DRIED FLOWERS, AND FOLK-ART FISH DECOYS COMPLETE THE ONE-OF-A-KIND LOOK.

Right: WITH A FEW OUTSTANDING PIECES OF ART AND FURNITURE, A FAMILY ROOM CAN RETAIN A CALMING AMBIENCE AND STILL PROJECT THE PERSONALITIES OF THOSE WHO LIVE WITHIN IT. THIS ROOM HINGES ON THE PAINTING AND COFFEE TABLE, WITH THE REMAINDER OF THE DECOR REINFORCING THE IMPORTANCE OF THOSE PIECES.

Right: THIS FAMILY ROOM PROJECTS ITS OWNERS' PERSONALITIES AT A GLANCE. THE PLATE COLLECTION SPANS THE FULL WIDTH OF TWO SHELVES AT THE CEILING, FRAMING, ALONG WITH SHELVES OF BOOKS, AN ART COLLECTION IN THE CENTER OF THE WALL. THE VIBRANT RED PALETTE PROVIDES A STIMULATING ATMOSPHERE, ACTUALLY INCREASING THE ADRENALINE OF THOSE WITHIN THE ROOM.

Left: ESSENTIALLY ARCHITECTURAL IN CHARACTER, THIS FAMILY ROOM WITTILY ESTABLISHES THE OWNER'S PASSION FOR THE CLASSICS. FROM THE CHAUCERIAN LINES STENCILED AROUND THE PERIMETER TO THE CUSTOM-DESIGNED NEOCLASSICAL BOOKSHELVES, THIS ROOM'S DESIGN IS A LIGHTHEARTED EXPRESSION OF A FAMILY'S LOVE OF LITERATURE.

Below: CONTEMPORARY ARCHITECTURE AND FURNISHINGS MERGE WITH PRIMITIVE COLLECTIBLES IN THIS FAMILY ROOM TO EXPRESS THE RANGE OF ITS OWNERS' INTERESTS.

Above: THE FAMILY ROOM CAN BE A SHOWCASE FOR DISPLAYING ANY ARRAY OF OBJECTS THAT HAVE SPECIAL MEANING FOR THE HOME OWNERS. THESE MINIATURE CHINA CUPS AND SAUCERS ARE THE RESULT OF YEARS OF COLLECTING. ARTFULLY PRESENTED ON ANTIQUE SHELVES INSET IN BARNBOARD PANELING, THE DISPLAY EXPRESSES A SINGULAR STYLE. **Opposite:** WHEN READING IS THE FAMILY PASSION, THE FAMILY ROOM BECOMES A REPOSITORY FOR THAT FAVORITE RECREATION. IN LIBRARY FASHION, SHELVES TOWER UP THE ELONGATED WINDOWS OF THIS FAMILY ROOM, MERITING A LADDER AND A SMALL LIBRARY TABLE FOR THOROUGH CONSUMPTION.

Right: MORE THAN AN ASSEMBLAGE OF FURNITURE AND ACCESSORIES, THIS FAMILY ROOM REVEALS ITS OWNERS' ATTENTION TO PLANNING AND DETAIL WITH A SERIES OF BUILT-IN, CANTILEVERED FLOOR-TO-CEILING CABINETS WITH PANELS DECORATED WITH ABSTRACT CUTOUTS REMINISCENT OF MATISSE. THE TWO FAR CUPBOARDS FEATURE OPEN SHELVING AT THE TOP FOR DISPLAYING BOOKS AND COLLECTIBLES, WHILE THE CLOSED CENTER CABINET HOUSES ELECTRONICS EQUIPMENT.

Left: THE MORE DIVERSE THE INTERESTS AND TRAVELS OF THE HOME OWNERS, THE MORE PERSONAL AND INTERESTING THE FAMILY ROOM. ORGANIZATION IS THE KEY TO SUCCESS IN AMASSING SO MANY DIVERGENT OBJECTS IN A SINGLE SPACE: ADEQUATE SHELVING ALLOWS A SINGLE, HUGE DISPLAY, WITH THE OBJECTS THEMSELVES ARRANGED LIKE A STILL LIFE WITH ATTENTION TO BALANCE AND SCALE.

Above: A LEADED GLASS WINDOW BEARING A COAT OF ARMS IS THE FIRST SIGN OF THE PERSONAL TOUCH THAT

GIVES THIS FAMILY ROOM ITS UNIQUE CHARACTER. A COLLECTION OF PHOTOGRAPHS IN CONTEMPORARY BLACK FRAMES PROPPED AGAINST

THE WALL AND UPON THE FLOOR MANIFESTS A CASUAL SPIRIT.

Opposite: WHEN THE PARTICULAR FORM OF THE FAMILY ROOM IS A GREAT ROOM, THE CAPACIOUS SQUARE FOOTAGE AND VOLUMINOUS VERTICAL SPACE OF THAT TERRITORY PRESENT A UNIQUE OPPORTUNITY TO PACK A MULTITUDE OF PERSONALITY INTO A SINGLE SPACE. IN ADDITION TO THE TELLING PIECES THAT FURNISH THE ROOM AND DECORATE THE WALLS, THIS SPACE'S NARRATIVE EVEN EXTENDS TO THE CEILING, WHERE AN UPTURNED CANOE TELLS A STORY OF THE GREAT OUTDOORS. **Below:** A PENCHANT FOR SCULPTURE, FOLK ART, AND BOOKS, AS WELL AS A SENSE OF THE MACABRE (AS ILLUSTRATED BY THE SKELETON SCULPTURE), ARE ALL REFLECTED IN THIS UNIQUE FAMILY ROOM THAT BRILLIANTLY BREAKS THE COOKIE-CUTTER MOLD OF FORMULAIC DECORATING.

Above: EVERY ELEMENT IN THIS FAMILY ROOM, FROM THE RICHLY PATTERNED PILLOWS AND UPHOLSTERY FABRICS TO THE GEOMETRIC-PATTERNED FLOORING AND FLAG COFFEE TABLE, MAKES A BOLD STATEMENT IN DEFENSE OF HIGH VISIBILITY. WITH ITS HISTORICAL TOUCHES, PLATES CROWNING THE DOOR-WAY, AND FISH PRINTS DRAWING THE EYE UP TO THE CEILING, THE ROOM PROJECTS VITALITY AND PERSONALITY.

◩ PART THREE ◩

BEDROOMS

JESSICA ELIN HIRSCHMAN

INTRODUCTION

Be it through myth or lore, tradition or ritual, history has grandly bestowed attention upon the bed and, by extension, the bedroom. The evolution of bed and bedroom design encompasses the history of science, art, and philosophy. Refinements in the look and feel of beds — and bedrooms — reflect advancements in technology, achievements in art, and changes in life-styles.

From its basic utilitarian beginnings, the bed has been the focal point of design development in the bedroom. Historical documents reveal that ancient Egyptian, Greek, and Roman peoples slept on well-formed bed structures. They draped animal skins and soft textiles over wood, stone, or metal frames to enhance comfort. Persian nomads slept on water-filled goatskins for the same purpose. The wealthy members of these societies decorated their beds with metal, ivory, wood carvings, and jewels to designate their privileged positions.

Such handiwork also reflected the particular significance of art and philosophy in ancient cultures. Egyptian pharaohs, who spent their mortal lives accumulating wealth and possessions for the afterlife, were entombed with several stately beds to sustain them through their postmortem journeys. Roman emperors decorated their beds and sleeping chambers with inlaid gold and carvings of animals that symbolized strength. These practices established the bed as both a design statement and a symbol of personal stature.

Bed height and embellishments such as canopies and drapes were also signs of wealth and privilege. For example, some Swedish farming cultures and European nobility shared a belief that the higher the bed stood off the floor the more successful and prosperous the family was and would continue to be. Similarly, bed size was also indicative of personal and familial stature. Until the eighteenth century, when room design and furniture became simpler and scaled down, bigger signified richer. In Queen Anne England, beds measuring seven by eight feet (2.1 by 2.4m) and eleven feet (3.3m) high were popular among those who could afford their high price tags. Layers of luxurious fabrics — satin, silks, velvets, gold-embroidered tapestries — draped canopies that soared as high as sixteen feet (4.8m).

Opposite: THE CASUAL CHARM OF THIS RESTFUL BEDROOM REFLECTS THE OWNER'S RELAXED LIFE-STYLE AND ECLECTIC DESIGN SENSIBILITIES. THE HERRINGBONE COTTON CANOPY IS DRAPED EFFORTLESSLY OVER A SUSPENDED POLE AND BALANCED BY A COUNTERWEIGHT, ECHOING THE ARCHITECTURAL DETAILS.

William Shakespeare immortalized one of history's most infamous colossal beds in his play *Twelfth Night*. The appropriately named "Great Bed of Ware," located at the Inn of Ware in England, measured twelve feet (3.6m) square and reportedly accommodated as many as sixty-eight guests at one time.

Perhaps the only period during which opulent beds and lavish bedrooms fell from favor was the Middle Ages. During this austere time, nobility and civilian alike slept on straw-filled sacks in fortresslike rooms. The emphasis was on personal survival rather than creature comforts. In fact, it wasn't until the sixteenth century that beds became somewhat permanent and warranted superfluous splendor.

Prior to that time, beds were disassembled, packed, and carried from residence to residence. Even draperies were boxed and transported to the new bedroom. (Reportedly, the practice of surrounding the bed with a curtain began during the Crusades.) As extravagant as some of these curtains were, they served the practical function of enclosing the bed for desired privacy.

In the sixteenth century, the advent of corner posts heralded a great change in bed design and bedroom decor. Beds were no longer collapsible. Four-poster designs eventually gave way to two-poster beds with heavy, intricately carved headboards adding even more prominence — and a permanent feel — to the bed and bedroom. These beds were more than de rigueur; Tudor headboards often brandished the occupant's coat of arms and other elaborate designs.

Exaggerated beds were just as popular in fourteenth-, fifteenth-, and sixteenth-century France, where the revival of art and style flourished throughout the Renaissance. Beds were constructed with as many as thirty textile parts and virtually no visible wood. Voluminous drapes, plumes, and fringed valances adorned state beds. After centuries of such opulence, however, eighteenth-century furniture design witnessed a dramatic change in the shape and construction of the bed.

English cabinetmaker Thomas Sheraton spearheaded a scaling back of proportions. Beds — and other furniture — became lighter and more refined. Simplicity replaced complexity. During this period, beds designed by such preeminent craftsmen as Chippendale, Hepplewhite, and Adams remained decorative but were smaller in scale. Materials also took on a lighter, more airy look as iron and brass-tubing frames came into favor around the middle of the century. Beds from this time and the

subsequent Empire period are still the primary models for many modern-day designs.

The *lit en bateau* — French for boat bed — was a particularly popular style. With high straight-backed ends, the design resembled a boat and inspired one of the most enduring of all bed styles, the sleigh bed. Introduced more than one hundred and fifty years ago, the American Empire sleigh bed was carved primarily from mahogany and featured matching scrolled headboards and footboards connected by low wood side rails. Its wood framing was reminiscent of a sleigh and was especially well suited for supporting the laced-rope mattresses of nineteenth-century beds. Whether traditional or interpretive, the shape of today's sleigh beds remains fairly true to form: blocky, low to the ground, and undraped.

In many ways, the history of the bed is the history of the bedroom. But as colorful as this heritage may be, it is not the whole story. Bedrooms are more than just display cases for ornate beds. They are the public expression of the most private self, a record of how each occupant chooses to live, relax, and partake in the cycle of life.

The photographs presented in this book were selected for their power to entice — and to revive the design and enjoyment of bedrooms. Approach this book not only as a captivating glance into sacrosanct, private worlds but also as a time capsule preserving the tradition of fine bedroom design.

Above: A SUBSTANTIAL CANOPY AND VOLUMINOUS DRAPES CREATE AN INTIMATE SETTING FOR A BED IN THIS UNUSUALLY LARGE ROOM. THE SAME HEAVY CANVAS FABRIC COVERS THE WALLS, AN EFFECT THAT VISUALLY SOOTHES AND ACOUSTICALLY QUIETS THE SPACE. BEYOND, THE FORMER SLEEPING PORCH SERVES AS AN ADJACENT SITTING AREA.

Bedroom Anatomy

Bedrooms are such wonderful places. To an adult, a bedroom is the private oasis that guards the soul, rekindles the spirit, and provides a sanctuary for tender abandon. To a young child, a bedroom is at once a playground, classroom, art studio, and keeper of all dreams. And bridging the bedrooms of childhood and adulthood is the sanctuary of adolescence, that very personal haven where every teenager seeks answers to—and refuge from—the mysteries of growing up.

Because bedrooms fulfill such a variety of emotional, psychological, and physical needs, their design must incorporate and reconcile numerous elements. They should be appealing to the eye as well as the mind, as beautiful as they are functional. Architecture, lighting, storage, flooring, wall treatments, and bedding ensembles—to name a few concerns—must all be considered in addition to the most fundamental element: the selection and placement of the bed.

It's been said that the position of a bed within a room says something about the habits and life-style of the occupant, specifically how he or she likes to begin and end each day. The Oriental philosophy of Feng Shui goes even further, relating the position of the bed to overall health and well-being. The principles of Feng Shui, as applied to the bedroom, hold that a badly placed bed will lead to restless nights.

Since the bed is usually the focal point of the bedroom, it often dictates how the balance of the room is furnished and used. Still, the bed need not be the overriding influence in bedroom design and decor, as evidenced by the following pictures. Personal tastes, individual life-styles, and even heritage often influence the look and feel of a bedroom.

Opposite: THE SENSE OF SAFETY AND ENCLOSURE IN THIS ROOM IS HEIGHTENED BY INTENSE RED LACQUER ON THE WALLS AND CEILING. THE WOOD BOX-STYLE BED FRAME BORROWS ELEMENTS FROM GREEK TEMPLE DESIGN. **Above:** A SOPHISTICATED, SIMPLE BALANCE OF COLOR AND PATTERN ACCENTED BY ANTIQUE WALLPAPER GIVES THIS URBAN BEDROOM A TIMELESS APPEARANCE BY DAY AND A RESTFUL, COZY GLOW BY NIGHT.

Above: USING THE SAME TEXTILE FOR ALL UPHOLSTERY AND FABRIC APPLICATIONS IS PARTICULARLY SUCCESSFUL IN A SMALL SPACE WHERE MULTIPLE COLORS OR PATTERNS COULD APPEAR OVERWHELMING. HERE, AN ELEGANT MAHOGANY BED FRAME AND MATCHING CROWN MOLDING RESTRAIN AN EXUBERANT ENGLISH CHINTZ. **Opposite:** IN THE EARLY 1700S, SOME TESTERS (CANOPIES) AND BED DRAPES MEASURED AS HIGH AS SIXTEEN FEET (4.8M). IN THOSE DAYS, THE SIZE OF FULL-LENGTH TESTERS AND LONG, HEAVY DRAPES REFLECTED THE WEALTH AND STATUS OF THE OCCUPANT. THIS PROMINENT BEDROOM IS FURNISHED IN ANGLO-INDIAN STYLE. THE CANOPY AND DRAPES ARE A TRADITIONAL INDIAN *IKAT* FABRIC; THE CONVERSATION AREA FEATURES A CUSTOM *RAJ*-STYLE TEA TABLE AND A VICTORIAN-STYLE LOVE SEAT. AN ORIGINAL NINETEENTH-CENTURY CARTOON WALL HANGING AND SILK MOIRÉ WALLPAPER FILL THE FAR WALL; SILVER LEAF PAPER ON THE CEILING CASTS AN ELEGANT SHIMMER ACROSS THE ROOM.

Left: EVERY ELEMENT OF THIS CONTEMPORARY BEDROOM IS DESIGNED TO TAKE ADVANTAGE OF THE BEAUTIFUL LANDSCAPE BEYOND, WHICH INCLUDES A SMALL-SCALE MAN-MADE LAKE. LOCATING THE BED AT AN ANGLE BENEATH AN INTENTIONALLY SKEWED SKYLIGHT AFFORDS A DRAMATIC VIEW AT SUNRISE AND SUNSET. JUXTAPOSING PRISTINELY FINISHED INTERIORS WITH AN EXPOSED CEILING CREATES THE ARCHITECTURAL ILLUSION OF A SPACE WITHIN A SPACE.

Left: USUALLY THE FOCAL POINT OF A BEDROOM, THE BED IN THIS SETTING RESTS LOW TO THE GROUND SO AS NOT TO COMPETE WITH THE DESIGN OF THE SPACE. A SIMPLE PATCHWORK QUILT PROVIDES THE BED WITH A SUBTLE PROMINENCE BENEATH THE HAND-PAINTED WALL. THE PASTEL COLOR SCHEME VISUALLY SOFTENS THE CONCRETE, WOOD, AND GLASS SURFACES.

Opposite: THIS *LIT EN BAL-DAQUIN*—A CANOPIED BED PLACED FLUSH AGAINST THE WALL TO FUNCTION AS A COUCH—IS DRESSED IN THE SAME HAUNTING SHADES OF BLUE AND GREEN THAT ENVELOP THE TINY ROOM. THE INTENSE COLORS, SET OFF BY THE RICH-TONED WOOD BED FRAME AND BRASS CANDLESTICKS, ADD DRAMA AND MYSTERY TO THE SPACE. SOME PEOPLE BELIEVE THE COLOR BLUE ENHANCES THE ABILITY TO REMEMBER DREAMS.

Above: IN AN IRISH CASTLE, SHADES OF DEEP BLUE HEIGHTEN THE CONTRAST BETWEEN THE RICH YELLOW WALLS AND VIVIDLY PATTERNED SHEETS. A REGAL BLUE DAMASK ADORNS THE CHAIRS. **Left:** MEXICAN ARCHITECT MARCO ALDACO ONCE EXPRESSED THE BELIEF THAT PEOPLE ARE MORE TRANQUIL IN ROOMS WITH CURVES. THE GENTLY CURVED BLUE WALLS OF THIS 1896 BEDROOM EVOKE A FEELING OF INFINITE PEACE AND QUIET.

Above: AT THE END OF A BUSY DAY, THE OCCUPANT OF THIS SUBDUED BEDROOM FINDS TRUE REPOSE FROM HER WORK IN THE VISUAL WORLD. THE MONOCHROMATIC COLOR SCHEME AND ABSENCE OF ARTWORK, SAVE FOR THE ILLUMINATED STARBURST, HELP CALM THE ROOM. **Right:** HAWAIIAN FABRICS TURN THE BEDROOM OF A 1950S CALIFORNIA BUNGALOW INTO A LUSH TROPICAL RETREAT. CURTAINS SEWN FROM *PAREO* CLOTH, WHICH IS TYPICALLY WORN AS CLOTHING, FRAME A BAMBOO BUREAU.

Left: TRADITIONALLY, JAPANESE FUTONS ARE BROUGHT OUT ONLY AT NIGHT AND PLACED ATOP TATAMIS—STRAW MATS THAT PROVIDE A BASIC FLOOR COVERING AND SOME INSULATION. BY DAY, THE FUTONS ARE ROLLED AND STORED OUT OF SIGHT. IN THIS PEACEFUL BEDROOM, THE BOULDER AND ROCK VASE REPRESENT THE IMPORTANCE OF NATURE IN ORIENTAL PHILOSOPHIES AND LIFE-STYLES.

Opposite: A TATAMI BED STANDS SERENELY AMONG MINIMAL APPOINTMENTS IN THIS NEW DELHI BEDROOM DESIGNED TO HONOR THE BUDDHIST TRADITION OF LIVING AMONG SPARSE SURROUNDINGS THAT ARE CONDUCIVE TO CONTEMPLATION. **Right:** ALTHOUGH THOROUGHLY MODERN, THIS LONDON BEDROOM BEARS THE DISTINCTIVE HALLMARK OF CENTURIES-OLD ORIENTAL DESIGN: PURITY OF FORM AND FUNCTION.

Right: WHEN THE WORLD OF FANTASY MEETS THE VISION OF A TALENTED SET DESIGNER, THE RESULT IS AN INDULGENT, MAGICAL BEDROOM FROM ANOTHER TIME AND PLACE. ON ONE DEEP RED WALL, A CURIOUS COLLECTION OF BRIC-A-BRAC AND POSTCARDS CREATES THE ILLUSION OF A FARAWAY SPACE AWASH IN INTRIGUE AND ROMANCE. **Opposite:** CROSSING THE THRESHOLD OF THIS VISUAL EXTRAVAGANZA IS LIKE STEPPING REVERENTLY INTO AN INDIAN PALACE OVERFLOWING WITH SILKEN OPULENCE. ACTUALLY, THE SHIMMERING FABRICS ARE INEXPENSIVE TEXTILES FROM THE DESIGNER-OWNER'S FAVORITE HAUNT: HOLLYWOOD BOULEVARD.

Above: A RESTORED, SPOOL-TURNED BED IS A FITTING CENTERPIECE IN A BEDROOM TUCKED UNDER THE EAVES OF A ROCKY MOUNTAIN LOG CABIN. A FEW CAREFULLY DISPLAYED PIECES OF CHINA PAY QUIET TRIBUTE TO THE FAMILY'S NEW ENGLAND ROOTS.

Opposite: AUTHENTIC FURNISHINGS PERSONALIZE THE BEDROOM OF AN AVID COLLECTOR OF WESTERN MEMORABILIA. HIGHLIGHTS INCLUDE A GENUINE 1930 MEXICAN SERAPE OVER THE PILLOWS, A MONTEREY BED FRAME, AND A CORONADO TABLE (TO THE LEFT OF THE BED). THE OCCUPANT ASSEMBLED THE LAMP FROM A CAST-OFF SHADE AND REAL STIRRUP.

Left: Nestling a bedroom, storage space, and adjacent bathroom into a small prewar Manhattan brownstone—with only one window—requires a lot of ingenuity. Here, glass blocks conceal the bathroom and illuminate the mezzanine-level bedroom. Cantilevered stairs appear to float along the wall, enhancing the room's feeling of openness.

Below: An improvised bunk bed assembled from painted industrial shelving serves as desk, dining table, china cabinet, and home office.

Opposite: This postmodern bedroom suite could easily pass for a spacious studio apartment. It's the top floor of a renovated urban warehouse. A custom-designed media center divides the space physically and visually. The "power tower," constructed from burled laminate with fuchsia accents, hides lighting and stereo equipment. The television swivels for easy viewing from either side. The same burled laminate finish is applied to the bed and custom-made combination headboard-desk.

Above: A REVERSIBLE EGYPTIAN COTTON DAMASK SWAGGED SYMMETRICALLY BEHIND A CUSTOM-DESIGNED BED TURNS A SIZABLE BEDROOM INTO A ROMANTIC BEDOUIN TENT. THE BED, MADE FROM POLISHED WHITE ASH WITH AN IVORY FINISH, FEATURES MINIATURE TURRETLIKE FINIALS ON ALL FOUR POSTS TO COMPLETE THE ROOM'S MOORISH LOOK. **Opposite:** APPROXIMATELY FOUR HUNDRED YARDS (365.7M) OF FRENCH PROVINCIAL PRINTED COTTON DISGUISES THE MODERN STREAMLINED ARCHITECTURE OF THIS GUEST BEDROOM. THE BED IS AN ORIGINAL LOUIS XVI PIECE, THE CHANDELIER ITALIAN, AND THE NEEDLEWORK RUG PORTUGUESE.

Opposite: Four-poster beds became popular in the early sixteenth century and have been at home in the bedroom ever since. Here, a traditional pencil-post bed and hand-sewn quilt capture the restrained beauty and timeless appeal of Shaker furnishings. **Above left:** Restoring an authentic ambiance often calls for a balance of new and old. Here, in an 1819 Federal period home, the custom-designed flat woven rag wool rug is new but the reversible jacquard bedspread, trimmed with a pattern called Old Boston Town, is generations old. **Above right:** The homespun jacquard coverlet draping this bed dates from the same period as the stone farmhouse. The furnishings, including a 1790 cherry linen press and handcrafted chairs, are typical of the eighteenth century.

Right: TO MAXIMIZE THE LIMITED FLOOR SPACE OF THIS SHARED CHILDREN'S BEDROOM, THE ARCHITECT CREATED A VERTICAL, MULTIPURPOSE BED SYSTEM WITH AMPLE ROOM FOR STORAGE AND DIFFERENT LEVELS FOR CLIMBING. STACKING THE BEDS IN THIS MANNER LEFT ROOM ENOUGH FOR A PLAYHOUSE AND CREATED A CONTINUOUS CANVAS FOR DECORATIVE PAINTING.

Left: CHILDREN NEED LOTS OF ROOM FOR CREATIVITY. THIS HIDEAWAY DESK AND PULLOUT AQUARIUM ENCOURAGE NEAT PARTICIPATION IN THE ARTS AND SCIENCES OF GROWING UP. POCKET DOORS CONCEAL THE BOOKCASE AND DESK WHEN NOT IN USE.

Right: THE UGLY DUCKLING, RUMPELSTILTSKIN, THE FROG PRINCE, AND OTHER CHERISHED FAIRY TALES COME TOGETHER IN THIS CHILD'S ROOM. THE MIXED-MEDIA MURAL WAS WORKED ON CANVAS THAT WAS STRETCHED AND SIZED TO COVER THE WALL. THIS METHOD, RATHER THAN PAINTING DIRECTLY ONTO THE WALL SURFACE, ALLOWS THE HOME OWNER TO CHANGE THE SCENE AS THE CHILD GROWS UP.

Left: KING ARTHUR'S FABLED KNIGHTS OF THE ROUND TABLE LIVE ON IN A YOUNG BOY'S ROOM FINISHED WITH A HAND-PAINTED SCENE OF MEDIEVAL ENCHANTMENT. ELEGANT FABRICS AND REGAL COLORS ADD TO THE MAGIC OF THE IMAGINARY CASTLE HIDEAWAY. TROMPE L'OEIL MURALS ARE AN ARTFUL ALTERNATIVE TO ORDINARY PAINT OR WALLPAPER WHEN IT COMES TO DECORATING AND PERSONALIZING A CHILD'S BEDROOM.

Above right: DECIDEDLY CONTEMPORARY AND CLASSICALLY ELEGANT, THE FOCAL POINT OF THIS APARTMENT BEDROOM IS THE EXAGGERATED METAL SLEIGH BED SHOWCASED ALONGSIDE AN ARTISTIC ROOM DIVIDER. **Below right:** AN ARCHITECT'S OWN WHIMSICAL BEDROOM REPRESENTS A PEACEFUL SETTING AMONG THE FRAGRANT CALIFORNIA ORANGE GROVES. MAJESTIC MOUNTAINS ON THE HEADBOARD AND AN ARCHED REDWOOD CEILING SUGGESTING A SUNSET-COLORED SKY COMPLETE THE FANTASY LANDSCAPE. **Far right:** MORE REMINISCENT OF AN ART GALLERY THAN A BEDROOM, THIS CONTOURED ROOM EXHIBITS RARE ARCHITECTURAL PRINTS, ORIGINAL ARTWORK BY THE OCCUPANT'S FRIENDS, AND A WIDE-ANGLE VIEW OF NATURE'S OWN HANDIWORK. THE CONVERTED HOSPITAL TROLLEY IS ITSELF A PIECE OF UNCONVENTIONAL ART.

Right: THE REMODELED ATTIC OF A VICTORIAN HOME WAS OPENED TO THE OUTSIDE WITH A CUSTOM-MADE SKYLIGHT AND BALCONY ADDITION. AN ORIGINAL ARTS AND CRAFTS WINDOW ABOVE THE BED, NATURAL WOOD ACCENTS, AND OAK FLOORING PRESERVE THE OLD-FASHIONED SPIRIT OF THE NEWLY RENOVATED SPACE. **Below:** THE ABILITY TO MOVE FREELY BETWEEN AN INTIMATE, SHELTERED SPACE TO ONE THAT IS UNPROTECTED AND PUBLIC IS A TRUE LUXURY. THE FRENCH DOORS LEADING TO THIS SECOND-STORY DECK OPEN OUT, RATHER THAN IN, TO EMPHASIZE THE FEELING OF UNINTERRUPTED SPACE BETWEEN THE MASTER BEDROOM AND THE OUTSIDE. THE DECK ALSO MAXIMIZES THE BENEFITS OF A YEAR-ROUND WARM CLIMATE.

Opposite: PERHAPS ONE OF THE MOST ROMANTIC, ENVIABLE ATTRIBUTES OF ANY BEDROOM IS A BALCONY. THE MAHOGANY-BALUSTERED BALCONY OFF THIS BEDROOM IN A SEVENTEENTH-CENTURY HOME IN THE ANCIENT WALLED CITY OF CARTAGENA, COLOMBIA, OVERLOOKS AN INNER COURTYARD AND FOUNTAIN. THE ROOM ITSELF STILL HAS THE ORIGINAL 1593 BRICK FLOOR AND TROPICAL HARDWOOD CEILING BEAMS, WHICH SUPPORT THE FLOOR OF THE ROOM ABOVE.

Above: EXPANSES OF GLASS ARE POPULAR ARCHITECTURAL METHODS FOR VISUALLY OPENING UP A ROOM. CENTERED AMONG SYMMETRICAL BLOCKS OF MEXICAN GLASS, A FIREPLACE INTRODUCES A SECOND KIND OF NATURAL WARMTH AND LIGHT TO THIS CONTEMPORARY BEDROOM. THE EYE-CATCHING MATERIAL ON THE FLOOR AND CEILING IS ORIENTED STRAND BOARD THAT HAS BEEN FINISHED WITH A URETHANE VARNISH. **Left:** FLOOR-TO-CEILING GLASS CAN CHANGE THE ENTIRE MOOD OF A ROOM AS LIGHT AND SHADOWS INTERACT UNPREDICTABLY THROUGHOUT THE DAY. HERE, AN INTERPRETIVE PINE CANOPY HANGS FROM THIN STAINLESS STEEL WIRES DESIGNED TO GRACEFULLY REFLECT INCOMING SUNSHINE AND MOONLIGHT. GAZING THROUGH THE OVERHEAD STRUCTURE AT NIGHT GIVES THE ILLUSION OF STARING INTO A DEEP BLUE, SPARKLING SKY.

Right: The only thing missing from this spacious master bedroom was a dressing area that would provide considerable storage without being too intrusive. The solution: a stepped storage unit built in front of the wall closets. The design adds unexpected dimension to the room's modern architecture, and the molding trim is repeated throughout the house.

Left: From the other side, the adjustable cubbies provide open storage for the homeowner's collection of shirts and sweaters and form a semiprivate dressing space.

Below: This contemporary urban home is designed on a grid. Various structural and design elements echo that plan throughout the house. In the second-story bedroom, a gridded screen partially separates the bed and dressing areas. The interlocking structure was fabricated from painted fir and galvanized steel pipe.

Above: The sleeping area of the bedroom plays out the home's gridded rhythm. The screen, which is repeated in the same spot one floor below, admits light from the big picture window beyond. The only noticeable break in the simple symmetry is two metal end tables that appear identical at first glance.

Above: TO CREATE A YEAR-ROUND GUEST HOUSE COMPLETE WITH A SLEEPING LOFT, BATHROOM, AND KITCHENETTE, NEW OWNERS RENOVATED A ONE-CAR GARAGE. THE SLEEPING LOFT IS OPEN ON EITHER SIDE TO THE MAIN ROOM BELOW, WHICH HOUSES THE BATHROOM AND MINIKITCHEN. THE ALL-WHITE COLOR SCHEME WAS SELECTED AS A SIMPLE BACKDROP—THE OWNERS RELY ON GUESTS, FOOD, AND SPARSE FURNISHINGS TO FILL THE TINY SPACE WITH COLOR AND TEXTURE. **Opposite:** POPPING UP THE ROOF ALONG THE CENTERLINE BRINGS IN CONSIDERABLE LIGHT AND EXTENDS THE HEADROOM IN THE SLEEPING LOFT. PERMANENTLY ATTACHED LAMPS PROVIDE READING LIGHT AS WELL AS SUPPLEMENTAL LIGHTING FOR THE LIVING SPACE. CLERESTORY WINDOWS ARE OPERABLE TO CONTROL VENTILATION.

Far left: THIS THREE-STORY APARTMENT DEFINES QUINTESSENTIAL LOFT-STYLE LIVING. THE ARCHITECT REFINISHED ALL OF THE SURFACES, SAVE THOSE OF THE ORIGINAL OVERHEAD STEEL BEAMS, AND CREATED A CYLINDER TO PUNCTUATE THE LONG WALL AND ANCHOR NEW SPACE ABOVE AND BEHIND. **Top left:** A BED IS TUCKED WARMLY BEHIND THE CURVED WALL. SELECT WOOD BEAMS WERE STAINED BLACK TO SIMULATE METAL. **Bottom left:** FROM HIS CIRCULAR MEZZANINE WORKSPACE, THE ARCHITECT ENJOYS A SWEEPING VIEW OF THE LIVING ROOM BELOW. A SWIRLING, SPIRALING RAG-ROLLED FINISH ACCENTUATES THE CURVED TOWER.

Opposite: The basic principles of solar design and the vernacular architecture of tropical Bali come together in this Indonesian bedroom. The partially uncovered ceiling acts like a sieve, allowing warm air to escape while also shading the room from intense direct sunlight. At night, stone floor tiles release stored heat to warm the cool air. The hand-crafted bed is mahogany, chosen for its natural resistance to termites. **Left:** A curtain separates the sleeping area from the adjacent bathroom. Bamboo mats and an antique painted wood vanity capture the regional style.

Above: THREE DISTINCT RUGS ADORN THE HARDWOOD FLOORS OF A GENTLEMAN'S NINETEENTH-CENTURY
AMERICAN EMPIRE BEDROOM. AN AUTHENTIC NAPOLEONIC CAMPAIGN DESK STANDS IN THE CORNER,
AND CHINOISERIE FABRIC COVERS THE BED. RICH JEWEL TONES SEPARATE THE ROOM INTO AREAS OF WARMTH
AND PRIVACY. **Opposite:** BEDS WERE ONCE VALUABLE FAMILY POSSESSIONS; AS EARLY AS THE FOURTEENTH
CENTURY, THEY WERE BEQUEATHED IN WILLS. THIS HEIRLOOM BED, EVOCATIVE OF THE FRENCH EMPIRE STYLE, IS
THE CENTERPIECE OF A TRADITION-LADEN MASTER BEDROOM IN A MEXICAN HACIENDA. THE BED'S LIGHT
AND FANCIFUL FRAME VISUALLY BALANCES THE ROOM'S OTHERWISE HEAVY FURNISHINGS.

PERSONAL TOUCHES

Bedrooms are extremely functional spaces. At the very least, they are a starting and stopping point for each day. For some, the bedroom is more. It may double as a dressing room, a home office, a library on a lazy Sunday morning, or an all-night private movie theater. For others, the bedroom might be a welcome respite to a hard day's work or a lovingly arranged homage to one's heritage and treasured family possessions. And then there are the many intangible functions of the bedroom: the sweet anticipation of a passionate encounter or the memorable magic of a childhood bedtime story.

Historically, too, bedrooms served more than their most obvious function. King Louis XIV actually conducted affairs of state from the bed in one of his many majestically appointed bedrooms (it's rumored he owned more than four hundred beds). Most great houses of the seventeenth century featured mourning chambers, bedrooms designed and decorated exclusively for receiving condolences upon the death of a loved one. Aristocratic widows and widowers reclined in beds draped with black curtains and covered in black silk sheets while friends and family paid their respects.

For both its noticeable and its subtle intent, bedroom decor requires care and contemplation. Equate designing and furnishing a bedroom with painting a self-portrait; because it is such a private room, its decoration affords an opportunity to indulge many design cravings. The following photographs offer a glimpse of some of the various furnishings and finishing touches that make the bedroom a truly personal space — and much more than simply a room with a bed.

Opposite: SHEER WHITE CURTAINS BILLOW LIKE SAILS ON A BED FLOATING EFFORTLESSLY ATOP A SAND-COLORED STRAW RAFT. IRON AND BRASS TUBING FRAMES ENJOYED CONSIDERABLE POPULARITY WITH MID-NINETEENTH-CENTURY BED DESIGNERS AND REMAIN A FAVORITE TODAY WITH TRUE ROMANTICS. Above: SHEER, DELICATELY PATTERNED CURTAINS AND A GATHERED DUST RUFFLE SOFTEN THE METAL FRAME OF THIS FRENCH CAMP BED. MATCHING THE SCALLOPED COVERLET TO THE WALLPAPER KEEPS THE ROOM INVITINGLY SIMPLE AND RELAXING.

Above: THIS SMALL GUEST ROOM WAS DESIGNED AROUND A WONDERFUL EIGHTEENTH-CENTURY PRINTED FOOTBOARD DISCOVERED BY ACCIDENT AT AN AUCTION. THE BED RAILS, HEADBOARD, AND WALL PANELING WERE NEWLY CONSTRUCTED AND FINISHED TO COMPLEMENT THE RARE FIND. EQUALLY UNUSUAL IS THE TWO-TIERED FRENCH SIDE TABLE, CIRCA 1930, WHICH WAS CARVED FROM ONE PIECE OF WOOD. **Opposite:** THE BEDROOM OF A WORLD TRAVELER AND PASSIONATE COLLECTOR BRINGS TO MIND MEMORIES OF FOREIGN JOURNEYS. THE INTERNATIONAL FURNISHINGS INCLUDE AN ORIGINAL LATE-NINETEENTH-CENTURY PAINTED PORTUGUESE TOLE BED AND LAMPS FEATURING GLAZED ITALIAN POTTERY. THE COLOR SCHEME AND TWO-TONE SILK TAFFETA CORONET CANOPY REFLECT RUSSIAN DESIGN INFLUENCES. THE PLANK FLOOR WAS CAREFULLY STENCILED IN AN ELABORATE PARQUET PATTERN.

Above: BEDROOMS, MORE THAN ANY OTHER ROOM OF THE HOUSE, SHOULD PAMPER THE SOUL. THE SKIRT OF THIS DRESSING TABLE IN A PORTUGUESE BEDROOM IS SEWN FROM A LUXURIOUS ANTIQUE BROCADE FABRIC. THE SAME FABRIC COVERS THE CUSHION OF THE ROOMY BENCH. **Opposite:** THIS REMARKABLY DETAILED TILE FIREPLACE OCCUPIES A CORNER OF A BEDROOM AT THE HISTORICAL STEDMAN HOUSE IN CALIFORNIA. IT IS DESIGNED AFTER SPANISH TILE FIREPLACES, WHICH WERE ACTUALLY TINY, DECORATED ROOMS WHERE PEOPLE COULD READ OR WORK NEAR THE FIRE'S WARMTH.

Left: A PADDED HEADBOARD UPHOLSTERED IN GLAZED ENGLISH COTTON CHINTZ IS ONE OF THE MANY COZY EMBELLISHMENTS THAT HELPS DISTINGUISH A CIRCA 1900 BEDROOM THAT LACKED ARCHITECTURAL DETAIL. PAINTED LINEN PILLOWS AND LAMPSHADES ADD A TOUCH OF WHIMSY; AN HEIRLOOM QUILT HEIGHTENS THE ECLECTIC LOOK.

Left: A TUFTED UPHOLSTERED BED, HEAVILY LAYERED FABRICS, AND MULTIPLE DECORATIVE FLOURISHES—CARRYOVERS FROM THE EDWARDIAN BOUDOIR—ARE REINTERPRETED HERE WITH CONTEMPORARY LIGHTING FIXTURES AND FABRIC-COVERED SIDE CHAIRS. THE BED FRAME UPHOLSTERY IS SILK COTTON TOILE.

Opposite: A YOUNG WOMAN MIGHT FIND THESE DREAMY SURROUNDINGS IDEAL FOR ROMANTICIZING ABOUT PRINCE CHARMING OR LIFE'S MANY SECRETS YET TO UNFOLD. A LACE-COVERED SATIN DUVET DRESSES THE EARLY AMERICAN BED; THE AUTHENTIC BUTTERMILK PAINTED BENCH IS OF THE SAME PERIOD. THE CABBAGE ROSE WALLPAPER IS ACTUALLY A NEW TEXTILE—APPLIED TO PAPER— INTENTIONALLY COLORED TO RESEMBLE OLDER FABRICS THAT WERE DIPPED IN TEA FOR A WARM APPEARANCE.

Above: THIS DELICATE BEDSPREAD WAS MADE BY TOPSTITCHING A COLLECTION OF VINTAGE HANDKERCHIEFS ONTO A STURDY SHEET. MOST OF THE HANDKERCHIEFS WERE PURCHASED AT GARAGE SALES AND FLEA MARKETS. TO COMPLETE THE DAINTY ENSEMBLE, THE OCCUPANT SEWED VINTAGE TABLE RUNNERS ONTO PILLOWCASES AND CHOSE A LAYERED EYELET DUST RUFFLE. Right: VIBRANT COLOR, ETHNIC PATTERNS, AND VARIOUS TEXTURES GIVE THIS MASTER BEDROOM A REFRESHING LOOK THAT IS AT ONCE COUNTRY CALM AND CONTEMPORARY COOL.

Opposite: FOR AN AVID ADMIRER OF EMPIRE AND REGENCY STYLES, THIS GUEST ROOM WITH ITS FAUX-GRAINED NINETEENTH-CENTURY SLEIGH BED AND HERALDIC FABRICS IS PARADISE. A FRENCH EMPIRE DRESSING MIRROR FILLS THE CORNER AND REFLECTS AN ANTIQUE CHINESE CABINET. A WOVEN DAMASK IMPROVISES AS A HEADBOARD. DIFFERENT WINDOW TREATMENTS ENHANCE THE ROOM'S ARCHITECTURAL DETAILS. THE WALLS ARE FINISHED WITH ALUMINUM LEAF SQUARES TO ACCENT THE SILVERY SUNBURSTS.

Above: IN TUDOR ENGLAND, HEADBOARDS WERE INTRICATELY CARVED; MANY DISPLAYED THE OWNER'S COAT OF ARMS. THIS ORNATELY CARVED AND EMBELLISHED HEADBOARD DISPLAYS PORTUGUESE INFLUENCES. **Left:** A FAUX-BAMBOO BED, DRESSING TABLE, AND TROLLEY LEND A STATELY POLYNESIAN ELEGANCE TO THIS BEDROOM.

Opposite: A CUSTOM-QUILTED SATEEN COTTON BEDSPREAD AND COORDINATED WALL PAINT TURNED THIS FORMERLY AUSTERE, INTENSELY BRIGHT ROOM INTO A REVERENT RETREAT. THE BEDSPREAD IS ADORNED WITH GREEN VELVET ROPE TRIM AND GOLD-EMBROIDERED SEALS FROM A ROMAN SHOP KNOWN FOR ITS PAPAL ROBES. A BUILT-IN WALL NICHE ALLOWS THE SPANISH SAINT OF GOOD EYESIGHT TO WATCH OVER THE OCCUPANTS, ONE OF WHOM SUFFERS FROM FAILING VISION. **Above:** SEVERAL LAYERS OF RANDOMLY APPLIED WATER-BASED PAINTS CONTRIBUTE TO THE DRAMATIC LOOK OF THIS DEEP RED BEDROOM. ADDING TO THE OLD WORLD THEATRICAL ALLURE ARE A TAPESTRY-STYLE BEDSPREAD, RUBY RED FULL-LENGTH CURTAINS, AND A FLOATING HEADBOARD, WHICH IS A WROUGHT-IRON GRILLE HUNG DIRECTLY ON THE WALL RATHER THAN ATTACHED TO THE BED FRAME.

Above left: FOR URBAN DWELLERS LIVING IN ONE ROOM OR SIMILARLY COMPACT QUARTERS, BEDROOMS ARE OFTEN SEEN ONLY AT NIGHT, WHEN A MULTIPURPOSE ROOM IS CONVERTED INTO A SLEEPING SPACE WITH THE TOSS OF A BLANKET. BY DAY, THIS IMPERIAL-STYLE, SILK-UPHOLSTERED MATTRESS IS AN ELEGANT, ANTIQUE-LOOKING COUCH. **Above right:** GRAY, BLUE, CREAM, AND TAUPE CERAMIC TILES PROVIDE A COLORFUL SPRINGBOARD FOR THE MONOCHROMATIC FURNISHINGS AND WALLS FAUX-FINISHED TO RESEMBLE PARCHMENT. OTHER UTILITARIAN OBJECTS TAKE ON ARTISTIC STATURE: OLD-FASHIONED HAND-HELD LIBRARY LAMPS PROVIDE PORTABLE TASK LIGHTING AND THE ONLY CHAIR IN THE ROOM IS DRAMATICALLY DRAPED WITH A WOOL PILE SLIPCOVER. **Opposite:** SPARE BEDROOMS ARE HARD TO COME BY. THIS ROOM OCCUPIES AN AWKWARD SPACE ON THE TOP FLOOR OF A MULTISTORY SEASIDE HOME. TO BALANCE THE UNUSUAL VERTICAL ELEMENTS, THE DESIGNER ADDED A TROUGH ALONG THE BASEBOARD AND A LOW MID-NINETEENTH-CENTURY-AMERICAN CAST IRON DAYBED UPHOLSTERED IN GLAZED SILK. THE SAND PIT—A BOLD USE OF FLOOR SPACE—AND LACQUERED RICE PAPER USED TO ADD TEXTURE TO THE FLOORING GIVE THE ROOM AN ETHEREAL QUALITY. THE BIRD CAGE IS AN AUTHENTIC EIGHTEENTH-CENTURY IRON SCROLL DESIGN.

Above: A GUATEMALAN CANVAS WALL HANGING, ORIGINALLY PAINTED AS A BACKDROP FOR A MEXICAN STREET PHOTOGRAPHER, TRANSPORTS A LOS ANGELES BEDROOM SOUTH OF THE BORDER. THE HANDMADE, ONE-OF-A-KIND NIGHTSTANDS FEATURE HAMMERED-TIN-CAN DRAWER FRONTS, GIVING THE ROOM A DECIDEDLY ETHNIC FLAIR. **Opposite:** A TROPICAL COLOR SCHEME AND GOLD-LEAF PALM TREE CAST AN INVITING LATIN RHYTHM OVER THIS LONDON BEDROOM. A RUG FROM OAXACA, MEXICO, AND ORIGINAL ARTWORK BY THE OCCUPANT'S FRIENDS DECORATE THE TRANSPLANTED PARADISE.

Top right: THIS
EIGHTEENTH-CENTURY
GUSTAVIAN-STYLE SWEDISH
BED RECEIVED A SPECIAL PAINT
TREATMENT TO SIMULATE AN
AGED FINISH; THE DESIGNER
FIRST APPLIED A WHITEWASH
OVER BLUE BASE PAINT AND
THEN TREATED BOTH WITH A
COMPOUND FORMULATED TO
MAKE THE PAINT SHRINK AND
CRACKLE. A QUAINT TOILE DE
JOUY COTTAGE PRINT ENVELOPS
THE HIDEAWAY. **Bottom
right:** VIBRANT-COLORED
SHEETS PROVIDE A STARK
CONTRAST TO THE CENTURY-OLD
WOODWORK FRAMING A
SLEEPING ALCOVE IN AN IRISH
ESTATE HOME. **Far right:**
WRAPAROUND PINE CABINETRY
CUSTOM-DESIGNED BY BEVERLY
ELLSLEY TRANSFORMS AN
ORDINARY CORNER INTO A
PRIVATE READING ROOM.
THE CAPTIVATING WINDOW
TREATMENT IS ACTUALLY A HAND-
PAINTED SHADE.

PART FOUR

BABIES'&
CHILDREN'S
ROOMS

CANDIE FRANKEL

INTRODUCTION

No sooner does a baby become part of a family than all kinds of new and unfamiliar objects start filtering into the home. Furniture, clothing, toys, and books—all geared to a young child's growing body and mind—play an important role in making the home a welcome, nurturing place. Containing the accoutrements of childhood and organizing them so that they are accessible is a challenge all families face, especially if space is limited or shared.

When children inhabit a room, the decor is never static or "finished." A child's fast-as-a-beanstalk growth calls out for space that is flexible and adaptable. Furnishings must be able to accommodate evolving interests, new hobbies, and increasingly sophisticated tastes without resorting to an expensive decorating overhaul every time a change is desired. Young children need space to explore lots of different art, craft, and play activities at whim. They love the sense of mastery that scaled-down furniture and easy-to-reach shelves and cupboards give them.

Older children find the most use for hobby and study areas, as well as places to entertain friends. They don't want their rooms to appear babyish or out of sync with their personalities.

CHOOSING AN APPROACH

Planning a room that will grow with a child requires meeting present needs yet always keeping an eye on ways the room can be adapted in the future. For budget-conscious families, this typically means a onetime investment in sturdy, functional, module-type furniture that can serve from infancy through the teen years and beyond. The same storage cubes that stack an infant's diapers, for example, can be used later to stow playthings, socks, or a comic book collection. Using plain, well-designed furniture as a backdrop for a child's revolving collection of clothing, toys, and school supplies is the most economical way to keep a bedroom up-to-date.

Opposite: THE RIGHT FURNISHINGS AND LAYOUT CAN MAXIMIZE THE SPACE OF A SMALL ROOM. WITH THE HELP OF A RAISED BED AND STRATEGICALLY PLACED SHELVES, THIS LESS-THAN-SPACIOUS BEDROOM CONTAINS ALL OF A YOUNG CHILD'S NECESSITIES, INCLUDING AMPLE FLOOR SPACE FOR PLAY, A DESK FOR PROJECTS, AND PLENTY OF STORAGE FOR BOOKS, GAMES, AND TOYS. VISUALLY APPEALING AS WELL AS EFFICIENT, THE ROOM IS FILLED WITH WARM AND INVITING COLORS.

The sheer volume of possessions children accumulate tends to focus attention on their storage needs, but that is only part of decorating story. Children live in a tactile world; they love to touch, hold, and handle, drinking in the essence of objects around them. Rather than keep precious objects off limits, some parents feel that childhood is the best time to get acquainted with antique dolls, toys, and other valued items so that children can learn to appreciate and care for them. How lavishly a child's room incorporates expensive or rare objects is really a matter of personal style, time, budget, physical space, and child-rearing philosophy.

Parents with a keen aesthetic sense need to keep in mind that the types of rooms children consider successful and desirable may not look comfortable or inviting to adults. Children are proud of their possessions and like to keep them visible and accessible, which often means that shelves appear as a jumbled display of shapes and colors. The strong appeal of playhouses, giant stuffed animals, and beds that look like cars can be bewildering to adults, but items like these can mean a world of fun and fantasy to children. To create a room that is acceptable to both you and your child, start where all designers do: interview the client.

INVOLVING THE CHILD

Talking one-on-one with a child about the room he or she envisions is the first step toward refining the ideas both of you have. Children can be remarkably matter-of-fact when asked direct questions. They will tell you what colors they like, how and where they want to store their toys and books, and which kind of desk surface they prefer. Almost all have a fantasy bed in mind that would make their dream room complete. Looking at magazine pictures and visiting furniture and home decorating centers together can help you both visualize the possibilities and see what's new in the marketplace. If necessary, your comments can steer a budding designer in the right direction. You might point out, for example, that black is rarely used for walls and ceilings, but that it can look quite dramatic in an accent piece such as a lamp or poster.

Don't be afraid to be realistic with children about space and budget restrictions. Once you have a basic idea of the room's furniture requirements, measure the room together and draw a floor plan to scale on graph paper. Be sure to indicate the placement of windows, doors, electrical outlets, radiators, and air-conditioning vents. Small color cutouts, also to scale, can represent chests, desks, bookshelves, and beds. Children will enjoy working

with the "helicopter view" that a floor plan offers, and they can move the furniture cutouts around in order to try out a variety of possible arrangements.

Rather than immediately reject a request for a special piece of furniture, go over the budget available for the project with your child. Explain what different aspects of the new room (furniture, linens, paints, wallpaper) will cost so that you can decide together how best to allocate the money. In order to spread out the costs or purchase a special piece, you may opt to postpone some parts of the project until later. Even children who are generally spendthrift will rise to the challenge of creating a balanced, workable budget to achieve their decorating goals, and they will gain practical experience in arith-

metic, handling money, and comparison shopping in the process.

Children lead such vital, creative lives that they are the natural source for insight into their own space and storage requirements. When fulfilling these needs, the adults responsible for outfitting children's rooms must strive beyond the merely decorative to achieve flexibility. The rooms on the pages that follow are as unique as their individual owners and reflect variables such as budget, space, and the children's ages and special interests. Some of the ideas are readily practical and attainable, while others are fanciful springboards for the imagination. All can be applied alone or in combination to turn any child's ordinary, so-so room into a spectacular place to live, work, and play.

Above: BUILDING THE DECOR OF A CHILD'S ROOM AROUND A POPULAR THEME OR STORYBOOK CHARACTER NEEDN'T COST A FORTUNE IF PURCHASES ARE CHOSEN JUDICIOUSLY. A COLORFUL POSTER AND A FEW STUFFED-ANIMAL FRIENDS (ONE BEHIND THE WHEEL OF A HANDSOME RED CAR) WERE SUFFICIENT TO ESTABLISH THE BABAR THEME IN THIS COLORFUL BEDROOM. AS THE CHILD MATURES AND INTERESTS CHANGE, THE WHITE WALLS AND CONTEMPORARY, WHITE DAYBED WILL FORM THE BACKDROP FOR A NEW LOOK, WHICH CAN BE ACHIEVED BY INTRODUCING A BEDCOVER, A WINDOW TREATMENT, AND PILLOWS IN NEW FABRICS AND COLORS.

WEE SPACES

Bringing a new baby home is such a special event that it's hard to resist setting up a grand nursery. Lavish canopied cribs, infant dressers, changing tables, and armloads of stuffed animals add so much charm to the new arrival's room, it hardly seems to matter that all these elements are quickly outgrown. However, while a separate nursery set aside for the new baby is always welcome, even families with space to spare often prefer to set up baby's area in the master bedroom for the first few months.

Despite popular buying trends, infants don't really need a lot of furnishings, clothing, accessories, or space to be happy. Most important are a sturdy, safe crib and, for parents and other caregivers, a comfortable chair for feedings as well as a changing table that is at a convenient height. Baby's clothing can be stored in armoires or other "grown-up" furniture, saving the expense of infant furniture that the baby will never personally use anyway.

White, ecru, and pastels are the most popular palettes for infants' rooms, but accents in bright primary colors are available too. Infants are more interested in light and shadow than in actual colors, so you might as well select bedding and accents in patterns you like while concentrating on keeping the room bright and cheery for baby.

The pages that follow show spaces that have been made comfortable and welcoming for infants and those who care for them. The ideas range from grand nurseries with every amenity to simple, cheerful setups in a spare room or corner. Each one is considerate of the basic needs of the wee ones who will call these places home.

Opposite: AN END OF A MASTER BEDROOM SUITE CAN BE READILY CONVERTED INTO A CONVENIENT, TEMPORARY NURSERY. HERE, A MIRRORED CHIFFOROBE PROVIDES ATTRACTIVE STORAGE FOR BABY'S LAYETTE IN MULTIPLE DRAWERS AND CUPBOARDS. THE PINK LOUNGE IS AS PRACTICAL AS IT IS ELEGANT, ALLOWING CAREGIVERS TO PUT UP THEIR FEET AS THEY FEED BABY. A WHITE WICKER CRIB HINTS AT THE GARDEN VIEW THAT CAN BE ENJOYED FROM THE SUNNY ENCLOSED PORCH ONLY A FEW STEPS BEYOND. **Above:** A FEW DECORATIVE EMBELLISHMENTS AND FURNISHINGS WERE THE SOLUTION FOR THIS OFFICE CONVERSION. FORMERLY A STUDY, THE STARK, WHITE SPACE WAS SOFTENED WITH THE ADDITION OF PALE, HAND-PAINTED RIBBON AND FLORAL MOTIFS ON THE WALLS AND FLOOR. FURTHER EFFORTS TO MAKE THIS ROOM MORE COZY INCLUDED REPLACING VERTICAL BLINDS WITH FLOWING WHITE SWAGS AND COVERING THE CRIB AND CHANGING TABLE WITH FLORAL-PRINT LINENS.

Below: ANGLING A CRIB NEAR A DORMER WINDOW GIVES BABY PLENTY OF NATURAL FILTERED LIGHT WITHOUT BLOCKING ACCESS TO THE WINDOW SEAT. AN UPHOLSTERED CHAIR, USED FOR SNUGGLING AND FEEDING, IS ALSO STRATEGICALLY PLACED, FINDING A COZY SPOT AGAINST A LOW WALL UNDER THE EAVES. THE PAINTED MURAL ON THE ARMOIRE DOORS PROVIDES AN EXPANDED VISTA IN THIS SMALL BUT PLEASANT ROOM.

Above: TWO ADJOINING ROOMS IN A MASTER SUITE, EACH OPENING ONTO A COMMON HALL, ARE INGENIOUSLY SEPARATED BY A CANOPIED CRIB. THE CRIB FITS PERFECTLY UNDER THE WIDE ARCHED OPENING BETWEEN THE PARENTS' BEDROOM AND SITTING ROOM—TURNED-NURSERY, MAKING IT ACCESSIBLE FROM EITHER SIDE. ALTHOUGH THE CRIB IS SITUATED IN THE MIDST OF TWO ROOMS, THE ABUNDANCE OF HANGINGS ON THE CRIB CANOPY HELPS CREATE A PRIVATE AREA FOR BABY.

Below: IN THIS MASTER BEDROOM, THE BASSINET IS POSITIONED SO BABY CAN GAZE AT AN ELEGANT GEOMETRIC STAR SUSPENDED IN A NEARBY WINDOW. SAFELY MOUNTED, THE GENTLY ROTATING STAR IS AS VISUALLY TANTALIZING AS ANY CRIB MOBILE. OTHER STARS ALSO APPEAR IN THIS QUIET, UNDERSTATED CORNER, LENDING A PLAYFUL TOUCH TO THE ROOM. A COUPLE OF TOYS ARE KEPT ON HAND NEXT TO THE BASSINET WHERE THEY CAN BE EASILY FOUND BY THE CAREGIVER AS NEEDED.

Above: CONVENIENT FOR STORING BABY'S TOILETRIES, A WALL-MOUNTED CABINET PUTS NECESSARY ITEMS AT ARM'S REACH WITHOUT CLUTTERING UP THE CHANGING TABLE. THE CLEVER HINGED DESIGN ALLOWS THE LOUVERED PANELS TO SWING OPEN AND OUT OF THE WAY SO TINY HANDS AREN'T ACCIDENTALLY PINCHED. A FEW FAMILIAR FRIENDS HOVER AROUND THE AREA TO KEEP BABY COMPANY DURING CHANGES.

Above: WHITE LAMINATED FURNITURE LINED UP AGAINST A NURSERY WALL CAN HELP TO

STREAMLINE AND OPEN UP A NARROW SPACE. THE MODULE UNITS CHOSEN FOR

THIS COMPACT BUT EFFICIENT NURSERY CAN BE REARRANGED IN DIFFERENT CONFIGURATIONS,

MAKING THEM A PRACTICAL INVESTMENT OVER THE LONG TERM.

Below: SECONDHAND FURNISHINGS FOUND LOCALLY DECORATE THE NURSERY OF A VACATION COTTAGE, SAVING A FAMILY THE TIME AND EXPENSE OF SHIPPING FURNITURE FROM HOME. BARGAINS INCLUDE A DISTINCTIVE WICKER DRESSER FOR STORING CLOTHING AND ACCESSORIES, A FRAMED DISPLAY SHELF FOR PLAYTHINGS AND CHEERFUL DECORATIVE OBJECTS, AND A QUILT STAND PERFECT FOR CRIB SHEETS AND BLANKETS. GATHERED FABRIC PANELS CAMOUFLAGE THE COTTAGE'S CRUMBLING WALLS UNTIL THEY CAN BE PROPERLY REPLASTERED.

Above: DURING A BEDROOM RENOVATION OR BUILDING PROJECT, THE NURSERY CAN BE RELOCATED TO A FAMILY LIVING AREA, SUCH AS A FRONT SITTING ROOM OR ENCLOSED PORCH. HERE, AN ANTIQUE CARRIAGE AND A STANDING LAMP WITH SHELVES HELP BLOCK THE ROOM'S WIDE FORMAL ENTRYWAY, MAKING THE SPACE MORE INTIMATE.

Opposite: A JUMBO YELLOW MOON AND COMPANION BLUE STARS PROVIDE AN INEXPENSIVE ANTIDOTE TO THE ALL-WHITE STERILITY THAT COMMONLY CHARACTERIZES AN INFANT'S ROOM. PLUSH, BLUE CARPETING ANCHORS THE SOOTHING COLOR SCHEME. WITH AN EYE TOWARD THE FUTURE, THE PARENTS AVOIDED CUTE NURSERY LAMPS IN FAVOR OF WALL-MOUNTED, SWING-ARM LAMPS THAT CAN BE USED WHEN THE CHILD IS OLDER. THE TRADITIONAL ROCKING CHAIR, PERFECT FOR COAXING BABY TO SLEEP, WILL ALSO RETAIN A PLACE IN THE HOME AT A LATER DATE.

Above: CREATING AN ENERGETIC MOOD, A PALETTE OF BRILLIANT PRIMARY AND SECONDARY COLORS KEEPS THIS ROOM BRIGHT AND UPBEAT, EVEN ON OVERCAST DAYS. COLORFUL DETAILS INCLUDE CRIB BUMPER PADS, CHAIR AND STOOL CUSHIONS, FABRIC WALL ART, AND PLASTIC DRAWER PULLS. THE IVORY WALLS AND LIGHT TAUPE CARPETING ARE UNDERSTATED AND NEUTRAL IN TONE, ALLOWING THE VIBRANT COLORS TO JUMP OUT.

Above: NATURAL WOOD AND WICKER FURNISHINGS ECHO THE COLORS AND THEMES OF THIS WILDLIFE MURAL. THE CRIB HAS BEEN STRATEGICALLY PLACED SO THAT BABY CAN SEE THE BLACK-AND-WHITE PANDAS UP CLOSE; THE SHARP CONTRAST BETWEEN BLACK AND WHITE IS KNOWN TO FASCINATE INFANTS AND HELP DEVELOP THEIR FOCUSING SKILLS. AS THE BABY GROWS INTO TODDLERHOOD, THE OTHER ANIMALS IN THE ROOM WILL BECOME FAMILIAR FRIENDS AS WELL. **Opposite:** THIS COORDINATED NURSERY SUITE HAS BEEN EASILY CREATED BY PAINTING OLD, UNFINISHED FURNITURE WHITE TO MATCH THE CRIB. AS NEEDS CHANGE, ADDITIONAL PIECES CAN BE REVIVED AND ADDED IN A SIMILAR FASHION. THE LIFELIKE BABY GIRAFFE, WITH ITS DARK, NATURAL TONES, STANDS OUT IN THE WHITE ROOM, PREVENTING THE ENSEMBLE FROM APPEARING BLAND OR WASHED OUT; THIS ENORMOUS STUFFED ANIMAL IS ALSO AN ENTERTAINING COMPANION FOR BABY.

WORK & PLAY

The bedroom of an active, inquisitive child is far more than a place to sleep—it also serves as a laboratory, library, art studio, study, backstage dressing area, and construction zone. As children undertake the serious business of play, they develop motor skills, embark on projects, role-play, and learn how to negotiate. The successful room functions as part workshop, part showcase. It gives a child the freedom to try all sorts of activities, to show off accomplishments and collections, and to pursue new avenues as interests change. When there is more than one child in the family, a shared playroom can provide many of these same functions.

Parents can help children get their rooms on the right track by providing large, smooth work surfaces and am-

ple lighting. Tables, desks, and chairs should be at a comfortable height appropriate to the child's age and size. Movable furniture should be lightweight so that children can rearrange it as needed or clear the decks entirely for an impromptu dance. For young children, the floor is an important surface for play. Hardwood or tile floors are best for blocks, puzzles, and toys with wheels, while plush carpeting invites sprawling out for reading or playing a board game.

The following pages reveal rooms that indulge children's special interests and hobbies, from doll collecting to space travel. Each one carries its own imprimatur and offers valuable ideas for display techniques, storage, work surfaces, and overall decor.

Opposite: Dolls, puppets, and stuffed animals are ready for imaginative play at a moment's notice in this toddler's room. The pale peach tint chosen for the walls and wardrobe is warmer than plain white, yet still functions as a neutral background for the room's eclectic collection. Child-size chairs and a rug with woven animal figures draw attention to the floor, where much of children's play occurs. **Above:** A large black bulletin board, ample built-in storage, and sophisticated midnight blue carpeting will usher the toddler occupant of this room into the student years with ease. In the meantime, there is plenty of room for both active and quiet play. The swing-gate crib will soon be replaced by a junior bed.

—

Left: A STEP-UP CARPETED PLATFORM PROVIDES A DISTINCT PLAY AREA THAT IS EASILY TRANSFORMED INTO A STAGE FOR REHEARSED OR IMPROMPTU THEATRICAL PERFORMANCES. GRACING EITHER SIDE OF THE THEATER'S CENTER AISLE ARE TWIN BEDS THAT PROVIDE COMFORTABLE SEATING FOR AUDIENCES OF ALL AGES. THE JABOT-STYLED WINDOW TREATMENT CARRIES OUT THE THESPIAN THEME, WHILE A NARROW PARTITION CONCEALS A SMALL BACKSTAGE DRESSING AREA.

Right: OUT-OF-THE-ORDINARY FURNISHINGS CAN INSPIRE A FESTIVE, PARTYLIKE MOOD IN A CHILD'S ROOM ALMOST INSTANTLY. HERE, A COLORFUL CANOPY IS DRAPED ACROSS THE CEILING, SUGGESTING THE FUN AND EXCITEMENT OF A VISIT TO THE CIRCUS. THE ROOM'S PROPORTIONS ARE TURNED ON END, ALICE-IN-WONDERLAND STYLE, WITH THE ADDITION OF TWO GIANT (BUT MAKE-BELIEVE) CRAYONS. A YOUNG ARTIST CAN SIT DOWN TO SOME SERIOUS COLORING IN THIS ROOM AT ANY TIME BY SIMPLY TEARING SOME FRESH PAPER OFF THE HANDY WALL-MOUNTED ROLL.

Above: RAINY DAYS AREN'T QUITE SO DISAPPOINTING IN A BEDROOM WITH AN OUTDOOR THEME. A STRIPED AWNING VALANCE, IVY-PLANTED WINDOW BOX, AND GARDEN-FRESH WICKER FURNITURE ALLOW YOUNG LADIES TO ENJOY A TEA PARTY ON A PRETEND PATIO. SHOULD IT START TO RAIN, THEY CAN ALWAYS RUN TO THE FANTASY-HOUSE BED FOR SHELTER.

Opposite: TRANSPORTATION THEMES REIGN SUPREME IN THIS LONDON BEDROOM, LEAVING NO DOUBT AS TO A YOUNG BOY'S MOST SERIOUS PASSION. THE FREESTANDING RED BUNK IS A FUN STAND-IN FOR A DOUBLE-DECKER BUS, PROVIDING HOURS OF ENTERTAINMENT, AS WELL AS A COMFORTABLE PLACE TO SLEEP, FOR OWNER AND VISITING PLAYMATES ALIKE. IMITATING REAL LIFE TO THE MINUTEST DETAIL, THIS FANTASY BUS TRAVELS A PAVED ROAD CLEVERLY SIMULATED BY A LIGHT GRAY CARPET INSET.

Above: A RAISED PLATFORM PLAYHOUSE AT THE OTHER END OF THE LONDON BEDROOM PROVIDES A SECURE HOME FOR A LARGE FAMILY OF STUFFED ANIMALS. LARGE PULLOUT DRAWERS AT THE BASE OF THE HOUSE STORE OTHER TOYS AND MAKE CLEANUP AFTER FLOOR PLAY AN EASY CHORE. BY INCORPORATING FAMILIAR SIGHTS INTO THE DECOR, THE ROOM MAKES THE REAL CITY SEEM LESS OVERWHELMING AND EASIER TO NAVIGATE.

Opposite: OVERNIGHT GUESTS ARE PART OF THE ROUTINE IN THIS LIVELY ROOM CONTAINING TWO BUNK BEDS. THE L-SHAPED CONFIGURATION ALLOWS A SINGLE LADDER TO SERVE BOTH UPPER BERTHS. SUSPENDED FROM HIGH RAFTERS, AN INDOOR SWING IS A DEFINITE VISITOR ATTRACTION. OTHER SOURCES OF ENTERTAINMENT, SUCH AS COSTUMES AND TOYS, AS WELL AS PERSONAL MEMEMTOS LINE THE WALLS AND OVERMANTEL, LEAVING THE CARPETED FLOOR FREE FOR PLAY.

Above: TO TONE DOWN AN INTENSE PRIMARY PALETTE, FABRICS WITH A STONEWASHED DENIM HUE FILL IN FOR BRIGHT ROYAL BLUE. USED ON THE WALLS AND BEDCOVERS, THE PALER BLUE TINT VISUALLY RECEDES, CAUSING THE BRIGHT RED AND YELLOW ACCENTS TO POP OUT. EXTRA FLOOR SPACE IS GAINED BY THE DOUBLE-STACKED BUNKS—A TIME-HONORED ARRANGEMENT WHEN SIBLINGS SHARE A ROOM.

Below: A WIDE PARTNERS DESK OFFERS A GENEROUS WORK SURFACE FOR THE SERIOUS STUDENT OR ARTIST. EXTREMELY USEFUL, THIS TYPE OF DESK PERMITS THE OWNER AND A FRIEND TO PULL UP CHAIRS ON EITHER SIDE FOR A MARATHON STUDY SESSION, AN INTENSE BOARD GAME, OR AN IMPORTANT CONSULTATION. THE DESK'S U-SHAPED END HELPS TO SOFTEN THE MANY ANGULAR LINES OF THIS BEDROOM'S SHELVES AND STORAGE UNITS.

Above: A PINE TABLE-AND-CHAIR SET PLACED IN FRONT OF OPEN VERANDA DOORS ALLOWS A YOUNG ARTIST TO ENJOY A SUMMER BREEZE. JOINING THE IMPROMPTU COLORING SESSION ARE SNOOPY (IN CELEBRITY SHADES) AND A CHINA BISQUE DOLL. ALTHOUGH THE HOSTESS HAS TEMPORARILY ABANDONED HER GUESTS, THE PLETHORA OF ENTICING CRAYONS AND COLORING BOOKS SUGGESTS THAT SHE WILL SOON RETURN TO FINISH HER MASTERPIECE.

Below: MODELED AFTER PROFESSIONAL DRAFTING TABLES, AN ANGLED, ADJUSTABLE WORK SURFACE GIVES A BEDROOM A CRISP, ENGINEERED PPEARANCE. A GRID BEHIND THE DESK CAN BE USED TO DISPLAY AWARD RIBBONS AND PHOTOGRAPHS, WHILE STEEL SHELVES ABOVE HELP TO ORGANIZE GAMES, SPORTS EQUIPMENT, AND HOBBY SUPPLIES. THE FLOATING-BED DESIGN AND RAISED DESK DRAWERS HELP THIS SMALL ROOM APPEAR LARGER BY EXPOSING ADDITIONAL FLOOR SPACE. AS POSSESSIONS ACCUMULATE, THESE AREAS CAN PROVIDE EFFICIENT, OUT-OF-THE-WAY STORAGE.

Above: PURSUING HOBBIES IN A SMALL ROOM IS MADE EASIER WITH AN L-SHAPED DESK LIKE THOSE USED IN PROFESSIONAL BUSINESS OFFICES. AN OBJECT OR PROJECT CAN BE PLACED ON ONE ARM OF THE DESK, WHILE A REFERENCE TEXT OR INSTRUCTION MANUAL RESTS ON THE OTHER. BOTH CAN REMAIN IN EASY VIEW AND BE CONSULTED WITHOUT FRUSTRATING RESHUFFLING. A FREESTANDING SHELF EXTENDS THE UNIT SHOWN HERE, GIVING THE OWNER A PLACE TO DISPLAY MODEL ROCKETS AND OTHER TREASURES.

Above: A WINDOWED ALCOVE LEADING TO A PRIVATE BATHROOM SUGGESTED THE PERFECT OUT-OF-THE-WAY STUDY CORNER. RECEIVING PLENTY OF NATURAL LIGHT, IT IS AN IDEAL LOCATION FOR HOURS OF DILIGENT STUDY. THE QUIET NOOK OFFERS A MEASURE OF PRIVACY, WHICH IS A REAL ASSET IN A WELL-ORGANIZED, SHARED ROOM SUCH AS THIS. AT THE SAME TIME, THE DESK'S BOLD RED COLOR SERVES AS A DECORATIVE PLOY TO HELP DRAW THE ALCOVE BACK INTO THE ROOM SO THAT THE SPACE DOESN'T APPEAR QUITE SO ALOOF. **Right:** WHEN A PRIVATE STUDY AREA IS NOT FEASIBLE, SEQUESTERING A DESK CAN BE AN EXCELLENT ALTERNATIVE. THIS SEMIPRIVATE STUDY AREA IS DEFINED BY A BACKYARD PLAYHOUSE, PAINTED WHITE AND BROUGHT INDOORS. WHILE NOT SOUNDPROOF OR COMPLETELY PRIVATE, THE SPACE DOES SURROUND A YOUNG SCHOLAR AND ENCOURAGE CONCENTRATION. CUT PAPER CURTAINS PRESENT A CHEERFUL WELCOME AT THE ENTRANCE.

Below: MANY WORLDS COLLIDE IN THIS COLORFUL ROOM, WHICH IS RIPE FOR FANTASY AND PLAY. THE FLOOR PLAY AREA IS DELIBERATELY KEPT FREE, ALLOWING THE ALTERNATING SOLID AND PATTERNED CARPET TO SUGGEST TERRITORIES FOR SUPERHERO ESCAPADES. A SCALED-DOWN VERSION OF A CLASSIC IRON BEDSTEAD AND A LOW TABLE WITH CHAIRS KEEP EVERYTHING GEARED TO THE LEVEL OF THE TODDLER RESIDENT. A THREE-STEP STAIRCASE, PAINTED BRIGHT RED, MAKES AN UNUSUAL TIP-PROOF NIGHTSTAND.

Above: ADULT-SIZE CLOSETS MAKE LITTLE SENSE IF TODDLERS AREN'T ABLE TO REACH THE ITEMS STORED INSIDE. IN THIS BEDROOM, THE DOORS OF AN UNDERUTILIZED CLOSET WERE REMOVED, AND THE CLOSET INTERIOR WAS TRANSFORMED INTO A CHEERY RED NOOK. THE NOOK PRESENTLY SERVES AS A BACKDROP FOR A PLAY KITCHEN BUT IT COULD JUST AS EASILY ACCOMMODATE OTHER PLAYTHINGS, SUCH AS TRICYCLES AND WAGONS, AN EASEL AND ART SUPPLIES, OR BOOKS ON LOW SHELVES.

Below: For now, this handsome upper-story space is used as a playroom, but it is destined for a glamorous future. The elegant window treatment, hand-painted cabinet, and rich carpeting are but first installments in the more traditional decor that will appear as the children outgrow their playhouse, toy workbench, and tiny table and stools.

Above: In two- and three-story homes, keeping tots away from stairwells is a serious challenge. One time-honored solution is a safety gate at the top of the stairs, shown here in an attractive picket-fence design that has rounded edges on top for safety. With the gate closed, the stairwell leading down from this sunny attic playroom is safely out of bounds, yet the open design allows youngsters to remain in full earshot of the floor below.

Below: Skylights bring much-needed light into an attic conversion that has only one window. This upper-story playroom relegates the children's activities and clutter on one floor of the house, away from the family's main living area. Rather than feeling banished, the children delight in escaping to their own private world. Plush, green carpeting suggests the soft, mossy earth found in woodlands.

Above: Encouraging children to develop their creative powers, the opposite end of this playroom features a puppet theater and child-size box office. The trifold partition is safely anchored and padded with carpeting. Providing plenty of storage for puppets and props, shelves and cubbyholes behind the partition extend the play area for young theater managers.

Above: THE SPECIAL REQUEST OF A LITTLE GIRL INSPIRED THIS PLAYHOUSE BED,

RENDERED FEASIBLE BY THE BEDROOM'S HIGH CEILINGS. REAL HOUSE DETAILS

INCLUDE GINGERBREAD SCALLOPS, LOUVERED SHUTTERS, AND A SHINGLED CEDAR ROOF.

COMPLETING THE OUTDOOR ILLUSION ARE A LANDSCAPE MURAL, A SKY BLUE

CEILING, AND GRASS-GREEN CARPETING, ALL OF WHICH BRING THE JOYS OF SUMMERTIME

TO EVEN THE COLDEST WINTER DAYS.

CREATIVE STORAGE

Ample, accessible storage is the key to creating a well-organized room that a child can keep tidy without an adult's prodding. Most children take readily to sorting and organizing tasks, but they usually give up when drawers stick or are too heavy, shelves are packed too full, or closet rods are too high to reach. Easy-glide drawers, see-through plastic bins, and stackable baskets are inexpensive items that show thoughtful consideration for a child's size, strength, and patience. Shelves positioned at a child's level are a must for books, games, and puzzles that are used frequently. Like adults, children function more efficiently when everything they need is well organized and at their

fingertips. Good storage lets youngsters move intently from one activity to the next and makes cleanup go faster, with less frustration.

Designing suitable storage requires analyzing a room's size and present furnishings, and mapping out possibilities for new storage on a floor plan. Even the smallest bedroom has underutilized space that can be tapped for its storage potential. The pages that follow show a variety of storage solutions, including dual-purpose furniture, under-bed storage, wire shelving, and window seats. Some units are built-in while others are freestanding. All dramatically increase storage space while enhancing the decor.

Below: SOMETIMES LOOKING NO FURTHER THAN A FURNITURE RETAILER'S SHOWROOM CAN YIELD THE STORAGE OPTION THAT'S BEST FOR A PARTICULAR ROOM. HERE, A PAIR OF TALL DRAWER-AND-SHELF UNITS FILLS IN FOR NIGHTSTANDS ON EITHER SIDE OF A TWIN BED, ADDING FEET OF WELCOME STORAGE IN AN UNEXPECTED PLACE. TO PREVENT THE UNITS FROM OVERWHELMING AND DWARFING THE BED, THE SAME BRIGHT RED HUE WAS CHOSEN FOR THE COVERLET. A RECESSED AREA BEHIND THE BED MAKES THE PERFECT NEST FOR A STUFFED-ANIMAL MENAGERIE.

Above: BUILDING A COMBINATION BUNK BED AND STORAGE PLATFORM IN THE MIDDLE OF A BEDROOM CREATED A MORE PRIVATE ARRANGEMENT FOR TWO SISTERS WHO SHARE THE SPACE. THE BUNKS OPEN OUT ONTO OPPOSITE SIDES AND AT DIFFERENT LEVELS, GIVING EACH GIRL HER OWN DRESSING AREA AND STORAGE FOR PERSONAL THINGS. KEEPING THE LINES OF COMMUNICATION OPEN, A WINDOW IN THE BACK WALL OF EACH BUNK ALLOWS FOR ACROSS-THE-ROOM CONVERSATION AND PROVIDES VENTILATION.

Above: A SLEEPING ALCOVE CARVED OUT OF A FORMER CLOSET MIMICS THE BOX AND CLOSET BEDS TRADITIONAL IN NORTHERN CLIMATES. SHELVES AT THE HEAD AND FOOT OF THE BED ARE PARTIALLY HIDDEN FROM VIEW, KEEPING THE MAIN PLAY AREA FREE OF CLUTTER. TO KEEP OUT EARLY-MORNING LIGHT OR SIMPLY TO PROVIDE SOME PRIVACY, A FOAM INSERT CAN BE SLIPPED INTO THE CRESCENT WINDOW FRAME.

Above: TWO CLOSELY SPACED WINDOWS IN THIS CORNER BEDROOM CROWDED IN ON A CONVENTIONAL TWIN BED, NO MATTER WHICH WAY IT WAS POSITIONED. TO RESOLVE THE FLOOR-PLAN DILEMMA, COMPACT, BUILT-IN FURNITURE WAS DESIGNED. THESE PIECES INCORPORATE BOTH WINDOWS INTO THE OVERALL DESIGN, FLANKING ONE WITH NARROW DISPLAY SHELVES AND GIVING THE OTHER A WINDOW SEAT WITH STORAGE. STURDY CROSS-BRACES JOINING THE BED'S TOPMOST RAILS LAY THE GROUNDWORK FOR UPPER STORAGE CABINETS TO BE INSTALLED AT A LATER DATE.

Right: AN INNOVATIVE BUNK BED ARRANGEMENT CAN MAXIMIZE STORAGE IN A LONG, NARROW SPACE. HERE, THE LOWER BUNK'S PLATFORM EXTENDS THE FULL LENGTH OF THE ROOM, PROVIDING A SMOOTH, FLAT PLAY SURFACE ABOVE A SINGLE BANK OF DEEP DRAWERS. THE SUPPORT STRUCTURE FOR THE UPPER BUNK PROVIDES STORAGE SHELVES IN ADDITION TO THE REQUIRED LADDER. ALTHOUGH MUCH ATTENTION HAS BEEN DEVOTED TO THE PRACTICAL EFFICIENCY OF THIS ROOM, THE AESTHETIC ASPECT HAS NOT BEEN OVERLOOKED. REFLECTING THE CHEERFUL SPONTANEITY OF CHILDHOOD, THE WALLPAPER AND LINENS SHOW OFF RANDOM, BRIGHT HAND- AND FOOTPRINT DESIGNS REMINISCENT OF A CHILD'S FINGER PAINTING.

Left: REACHED BY A SHORT, EASY-TO-CLIMB LADDER, THIS MID-HEIGHT PLATFORM BED PACKS LOTS OF STORAGE SPACE UNDERNEATH AND HOUSES A SIZEABLE LIBRARY ON SHELVES ABOVE. CONVENIENTLY LOCATED ONLY A FEW STEPS FROM THE BOOK COLLECTION, A COZY EASY CHAIR PROVIDES MUCH-APPRECIATED COMFORT FOR THE BEDTIME STORYTELLER. THE BED, OVERHUNG WITH A DECORATIVE CANOPY, HAS THE ADDED ADVANTAGE OF BED CURTAINS THAT CAN BE DRAWN CLOSED FOR COMPLETE SECLUSION.

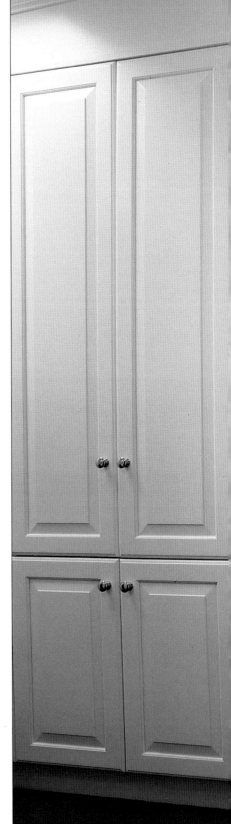

Above: A SLANTING CEILING THAT CUTS BACK OPTIONS FOR FREESTANDING FURNITURE OFTEN PROVIDES THE PERFECT SITE FOR A BUILT-IN DESK. HERE, THE BANK OF CABINETS SUPPORTING THE LONG COUNTER ADDS PRECIOUS INCHES OF STORAGE IN A SMALL BEDROOM, WHILE STILL LEAVING AMPLE ROOM FOR A DESK KNEEHOLE. WITH PLENTY OF SPACE FOR PAPERS, BOOKS, AND SCIENCE PROJECTS, THE VAST WORK SURFACE EASILY ACCOMMODATES A COMPUTER MONITOR AND KEYBOARD AS WELL. **Right:** ASYMMETRICAL BUILT-IN FURNITURE PREVENTS A BEDROOM ALCOVE FROM APPEARING STILTED OR PREDICTABLE. THIS UNIT INCLUDES A WARDROBE AND UNDER-BED STORAGE DRAWERS, ELIMINATING THE NEED FOR A SEPARATE DRESSER AND NIGHT TABLE. UP ABOVE, THE SLOPED CEILING RISES IN AN ARCHITECTURAL CANOPY.

Opposite: TIRED OF HAVING STUFFED TOYS DOMINATE HIS ROOM BUT NOT QUITE WILLING TO PART WITH THEM, A

YOUNG COLLECTOR HAS GATHERED THEM IN A JUMBO WICKER FRUIT BASKET. THESE CHERISHED SOURCES OF COMFORT

ARE AVAILABLE FOR QUICK HUGS WHEN A NOSTALGIC PANG TAKES OVER, BUT MOST OF THE TIME THEY ARE HIDDEN FROM VIEW

IN HIS NEWER, MORE GROWN-UP ROOM. **Above:** INSPIRED BY THE ROLLING CARTS USED ON FACTORY FLOORS,

TOY BINS ON WHEELS ARE PRACTICAL FOR STORING POSSESSIONS AND MOVING THEM AROUND A BEDROOM. AFTER PLAY,

YOUNGSTERS CAN ROLL AN EMPTY BIN OVER TO THE PLAY AREA AND PILE THEIR TOYS INTO IT, MAKING THE TIDYING-UP

PROCESS FAST AND UNCOMPLICATED. TO INCREASE FLOOR SPACE, EACH BIN HAS ITS OWN GARAGE BUILT INTO THE WALL UNIT.

Above: OPEN METAL SHELVING PURCHASED AT A KITCHEN SUPPLY STORE FORMS AN IMPRESSIVE STORAGE BANK IN A BOY'S BEDROOM. BOOKS, MODELS, AND STUFFED TOYS OCCUPY THE UPPER SHELVES, WHILE DOWN BELOW, RIGS ARE READY TO PULL OUT AT A MOMENT'S NOTICE. A TRIFOLD LOUVERED SCREEN GARAGES A FEW ADDITIONAL ITEMS BEHIND THE BED. **Right:** MUSTARD GOLD STEEL SHELVING UNITS PARTITION THIS LARGE ROOM INTO TWO DISTINCT AREAS. BABY'S SIDE IS SIMPLY FURNISHED WITH A STANDARD CRIB AND A CHEST THAT DOUBLES AS A CHANGING TABLE. JUST STEPS AWAY, A SITTING AND CRAFT AREA ALLOWS MOTHER TO PURSUE PERSONAL INTERESTS WHILE STILL BEING ABLE TO KEEP A CLOSE EYE ON BABY. COLOR-CODED PLASTIC CRATES, WHICH MAKE GREAT, INEXPENSIVE ORGANIZATIONAL TOOLS, LINE THE PARTITIONING SHELVES, STORING ITEMS FOR BOTH AREAS.

Above: BANKING ALL THE SHELVES ON A WINDOW WALL MAKES A ROOM SEEM LARGER AND NEATER. IN THIS

CITY APARTMENT, OPEN SHELVES BUILT AROUND AN EXISTING WINDOW HOLD GAMES, BOOKS, AND STUFFED ANIMALS. THE

WINDOW HELPS DRAW THE EYE OUT, PAST SHELVES THAT ARE POTENTIALLY OVERFILLED OR SLIGHTLY DISORGANIZED. BALLOON

SHADES AND A GAUZY BED CANOPY SOFTEN THE SHELVES' PRECISION GRID AND GIVE THE ROOM A COZY FEELING.

Below: PLASTIC STORAGE BOXES LETTERED WITH PERMANENT PEN KEEP THE SMALL BITS AND PIECES OF A YOUNGSTER'S VARIED COLLECTION PROPERLY SORTED AND CATALOGED. ADULT PERUSAL OF A CHILD'S ESSENTIAL CATEGORIES IS BOUND TO DRAW A SMILE AND PERHAPS A MEMORY OR TWO. THE BOXES ARE STACKED NEATLY IN AN OAK DISPLAY SHELF AND CAN EASILY BE RETRIEVED FOR CLOSE INSPECTION OF THE CONTENTS.

Above: A LIVING ROOM CORNER SET ASIDE FOR VISITING CHILDREN FEATURES A LOW BOOKSHELF FILLED WITH TOYS, BOOKS, AND GAMES. EVERYTHING STORED HERE ENCOURAGES QUIET PLAY AND INVITES THE CHILDREN TO AMUSE THEMSELVES WHILE THE GROWN-UPS ARE TALKING.

Opposite: PUTTING A COLLECTION ON FULL DISPLAY IS ONE WAY TO RESOLVE A STORAGE DILEMMA. FOLK ART CRITTERS, A CHILD'S PERSONAL ARTWORK, AND FAMILY PHOTOS ARE AMONG THE MANY TREASURED ITEMS MOUNTED ON WALLS AND PERCHED ON SHELVES THROUGHOUT THIS LIVELY BEDROOM-TURNED–ART GALLERY. ADDITIONAL ITEMS ARE REFLECTED IN THE MIRROR ABOVE THE HEADBOARD.

Above: A JACKET AND SNEAKERS WORN EVERY DAY ARE EASILY FOUND HANGING OUT IN THE OPEN ON A PEGBOARD. NO PLAIN BOARD MODEL, THIS CRESCENT-SHAPED MAN-IN-THE-MOON PEGBOARD WAS CUT ON A JIGSAW AND HAND-PAINTED. CONTINUING THE CELESTIAL THEME, THE PALE BLUE WALL IS STENCILED AT RANDOM WITH WHITE STARS.

Above: ROBIN'S-EGG BLUE, A TRADITIONAL COLOR FOR CABINET INTERIORS, PERKS UP A BANK OF SERVICEABLE WHITE CABINETS AND ACCENTS THEIR DEPTH. ALTHOUGH THE STORAGE SPACE PROVIDED HERE IS AMPLE, MOST OF THE CONTENTS REMAIN HIDDEN FROM VIEW, A SENSIBLE APPROACH IN A SMALL ROOM THAT COULD EASILY BE OVERWHELMED BY TOO BUSY A DISPLAY. **Opposite:** LOOKING MORE LIKE A CASTLE THAN A STORAGE UNIT, THIS PIECE OF BEDROOM FURNITURE MAKES A GAME OUT OF TAKING OBJECTS OUT AND PUTTING THEM AWAY. THE CABINET DOORS SWING OPEN BY PULLING ON THE EASY-TO-SEE BAR HANDLES, BUT TODDLERS CAN ALSO REACH IN THROUGH THE RECTANGULAR AND ARCHED CUTOUT OPENINGS TO RETRIEVE WANTED TOYS. IN THE MIDDLE SECTION, OPEN SHELVES STORE ASSORTED TOYS IN FULL VIEW AND OFFER A SHELTERED DISPLAY AREA FOR WOODEN BLOCKS. SINCE CHILDREN CANNOT REACH THE TOP COMPARTMENTS, THESE AREAS ARE BEST RESERVED FOR SEASONAL TOYS AND CLOTHES.

GROWING UP

The threshold into young adulthood is never crossed overnight, though it may seem that way to a lot of parents. The bedrooms of older children are often curious mixtures of old and new, reflecting a stage of transition. Stuffed animals and other comforting reminders of childhood mingle freely with sophisticated electronic equipment, sports paraphernalia, and celebrity posters. These are the years to pursue childhood interests in greater depth as well as to daydream and prepare for the future.

An increased need for privacy, a quiet, well-equipped study area, and room to entertain friends are all important aspects of an adolescent's world. The ideal bedroom functions like a small suite, giving independence and total privacy when desired yet remaining steps away from the hub of family activities. Newly developed tastes may lead an older child to demonstrate considerable decorating savvy when it comes to pursuing the colors, lighting, and furnishings needed for a particular ambience. The pages that follow contain ideas for surface finishes, window treatments, bedding, storage, and displays that can make any adolescent's room a haven from the world as well as a preparation for it.

Opposite: SHADES OF LAVENDER, PURPLE, AND ROSE CREATE A REGAL PALACE FOR A PETITE PRINCESS. THE BOUDOIR CHAIR IS AN ORDINARY DESK CHAIR DRAPED WITH PURPLE FABRIC AND FINISHED WITH A POUFY KNOT. THE LOW L-SHAPED DESK WITH ITS BAROQUE MIRROR IS JUST AS LIKELY TO BE USED FOR COLORING AS FOR APPLYING LIPSTICK BEFORE A DANCE RECITAL. A LATERAL FILE CABINET THAT HAS BEEN SPONGED SMOKY GRAY STORES VALUABLE POSSESSIONS UNDER LOCK AND KEY. **Above:** INDULGING A YOUNG PERSON'S INTEREST IN HISTORICAL OBJECTS CAN HELP FOSTER A LIFELONG APPRECIATION. THE OCCUPANT OF THIS BEDROOM IS THRILLED TO BE SLEEPING ON AN OLD IRON BEDSTEAD WITH AN ANTIQUE COUNTERPANE AND PATCHWORK QUILT. THE FLOWERY DECOR KEEPS THE FEELING OF SPRING ALIVE THROUGHOUT THE YEAR.

Below: A GIRL'S FIRST TRADITIONAL BEDROOM SUITE, SELECTED FROM THE JUVENILE DEPARTMENT, IS SCALED SLIGHTLY SMALLER THAN ADULT FURNITURE TO SUIT HER STILL-GROWING FRAME. THE FRENCH BED, WHICH FACES INTO THE ROOM LIKE A COUCH, GIVES THE ROOM THE AURA OF A LADY'S PARLOR. LOUVERED SHUTTERS EXTEND BELOW THE WINDOW TO SKILLFULLY SCREEN AN UNATTRACTIVE HEATING VENT.

Above: A BEDROOM IN A FAMILY'S CONDOMINIUM HOME SEEMS MORE LIKE A STUDIO APARTMENT, GIVING A DAUGHTER A FIRST TASTE OF LIFE ON HER OWN. THE PAINTED CUPBOARD, UPHOLSTERED ARMCHAIR, AND COUNTRY-STYLE DAYBED ARE ALL INVESTMENT PIECES WITH A BRIGHT FUTURE. THE YOUNG LADY CAN TAKE THEM WITH HER TO A FUTURE HOME, OR THEY CAN REMAIN BEHIND TO FURNISH HER PARENTS' NEW GUEST ROOM.

Above: GROWN-UP AND JUVENILE TOUCHES INTERMINGLE FREELY IN THIS

ADOLESCENT'S ROOM, CREATING ITS ESSENTIAL CHARM. AT THE MOMENT, THREE SPRIGHTLY

BUNNIES PEEK OVER THE PILLOWS OF THE YOUNG PERSON'S BED. THESE CUTE

ANIMALS ARE BOUND TO DISAPPEAR IN A FEW YEARS' TIME, BUT THE BEAUTIFUL DRESSING

TABLE AND LONG ROSE DRAPES WILL LOOK AS ELEGANT AS EVER.

Above: The children's guest room at grandma's house lets siblings and cousins room together in one happy dormitory. Plaid flannel sheets and matching dust ruffles coordinate the mismatched beds, which were gathered together from various quarters. There's plenty of room on the floor for overflow guests who bring their sleeping bags.

Below: A PAINTED BEDROOM SET, ROSEBUD PRINT WALLPAPER, AND A FLORAL CARPET ENVELOP THIS ROOM WITH FEMININITY. POSITIONED NEAR THE WINDOW, AN UPHOLSTERED CHAISE LONGUE PERMITS RELAXED READING OR INDULGENT SNOOZES WITHOUT WORRY OF MUSSING UP THE BED. THE SWIVEL MIRROR'S SPIRE TOP IS A CONVENIENT SPOT FOR DISPLAYING THE OWNER'S FLOWER-TRIMMED HAT BETWEEN OUTINGS.

Above: FINDING PRIVACY TO SOCIALIZE WITH FRIENDS IS A SPECIAL NEED OF OLDER CHILDREN, ESPECIALLY WITHIN THE CONFINES OF A CITY APARTMENT. DAYBEDS TRANSFORM THIS BEDROOM INTO A SELF-CONTAINED SITTING ROOM. THEIR PLACEMENT OPPOSITE EACH OTHER FACILITATES CONVERSATION, WHILE THE PRESENCE OF A SECOND BED ALSO ALLOWS FOR AN OVERNIGHT GUEST. ASIDE FROM PROVIDING A WELL-LIT STUDY SPOT, THE LONG DESK COUNTER AT THE WINDOW CAN BE USED AS A BUFFET FOR REFRESHMENTS.

Opposite: A TENTLIKE DRAPE OVER A SCANDINAVIAN BOX BED PROVIDES THE SAME PLEASURE AS A CONVENTIONAL CANOPY BED. HIGH CEILINGS MAKE THE TENT EXCEPTIONALLY LOFTY, BUT THE SAME IDEA CAN BE ADAPTED FOR A CEILING OF LOWER HEIGHT AS WELL. THE ENTIRE ROOM IS SPARE AND SIMPLE, EVIDENCE OF A YOUNG PERSON'S MATURING TASTES.

Above: A DIMINUTIVE VANITY CAN BE THE FAVORITE SPOT OF A YOUNG GIRL EMBARKING UPON ADOLESCENCE, EXPERIMENTING WITH MAKEUP AND HAIRSTYLES. HAVING SPECIAL DRAWERS TO STORE JEWELRY, COSMETICS, AND TRINKETS IS NOT ONLY FUN, BUT HELPFUL IN KEEPING AN OTHERWISE TIDY ROOM FREE OF MISCELLANEOUS CLUTTER. PERCHED ON A NEARBY RADIATOR, A BELOVED CHIMP REMINDS ALL WHO ENTER THAT THIS STAGE OF LIFE IS NOT A COMPLETE DEPARTURE FROM CHILDHOOD, BUT RATHER A PERIOD OF TRANSITION.

Opposite: When an older child's twin bed is replaced by a double, it may take a little work to accommodate the new, larger piece of furniture. Here, the space problem has been resolved by backing an antique desk against the foot of a double bed, allowing both pieces to fit in the narrow bedroom. **Above:** A twin bed, a nightstand, and open shelving for books and trophies are predictable furnishings in an active boy's room. The surprise feature is the deep shade of blue that covers the walls, creating an air of boldness. Cleverly masking uneven edges at the ceiling line, a sports-minded wallpaper border runs around the room.

Above: FOR A BOY WHO'D RATHER BE CAMPING THAN STUDYING, A BEDROOM WALL PAINTED WITH NATURE MURALS IS THE NEXT BEST THING. A REALISTIC WETLANDS SCENE AND TWO LEAFY TREES PROVIDE IMMEDIATE AMBIENCE RIGHT AT HOME. THE EXTRA PATTERN AND COLOR THAT A MURAL SUPPLIES HELP TO MAKE A SIMPLY FURNISHED ROOM APPEAR MORE DYNAMIC WITHOUT INTRODUCING OBJECTS THAT WOULD CLUTTER THE SPACE. **Right:** TROMPE L'OEIL PAINTING TURNS AN ORDINARY BEDROOM INTO A LOG CABIN INTERIOR. THE DECEPTION EXTENDS TO A RUGGED DENIM JACKET HANGING ON THE DOOR AND A DISHEVELED BOOKCASE. IN KEEPING WITH THE RUSTIC THEME, TWIN BEDS ARE APPROPRIATELY DRESSED IN LUMBERJACK'S PLAID FLANNEL.

Opposite: THE SHEER SIZE OF THIS SHARED ROOM ORIGINALLY OVERWHELMED THE TWIN BEDS AND MADE THEM SEEM BORING AND BARRACKLIKE. TO BREAK UP THE RECTILINEAR MONOTONY, THE BEDS WERE TURNED ON AN ANGLE AND TOPPED WITH EYE-POPPING BLACK-AND-WHITE SPREADS. THE NEW ARRANGEMENT STILL LEAVES PLENTY OF FLOOR SPACE FOR ROLL-IN BICYCLE STORAGE. **Above left:** BUILT-IN FURNITURE TAKES THE EDGE OFF A SPACE CRUNCH IN A YOUNG TEENAGER'S SMALL BEDROOM. INSTEAD OF GOBBLING UP PRECIOUS FLOOR SPACE LIKE A TRADITIONAL DRESSER, A TRIANGULAR CORNER CLOSET STACKED WITH SHELVES STORES THE TEEN'S EXTENSIVE WARDROBE ON A VERTICAL AXIS. TO FACILITATE MOVEMENT WITHIN THE ROOM, THE CLOSET'S TRIANGULAR FOOTPRINT PERMITS A CLEAR, WIDE PATH TO THE WINDOWED STUDY AREA INCORPORATED BEHIND THE PARTITION. USED FOR SLEEPING AS WELL AS LOUNGING, A CARPETED PLATFORM TOPPED BY A SINGLE MATTRESS VISUALLY EXTENDS THE FLOOR SURFACE IN THIS COMPACT, WELL-ORGANIZED SPACE. **Above right:** STREAMLINED CONTEMPORARY FURNISHINGS—BED, DESK, CREDENZA, DRESSER, AND LOUNGE CHAIRS—SUIT A BOY'S BACHELOR IMAGE. TO PRESERVE THE ROOM'S CLEAN, SLEEK STYLE, SUPERFLUOUS ITEMS ARE STORED RATHER THAN DISPLAYED, LEAVING PLENTY OF UNCLUTTERED SPACE FOR ENTERTAINING GUESTS. A YOUNG HOST CAN QUICKLY AND EASILY SET UP GUEST BEDS FOR HIS OVERNIGHT VISITORS BY UNFOLDING EACH LOW-SLUNG, DUAL-PURPOSE LOUNGE CHAIR INTO A TWIN-SIZE MATTRESS.

A Child's Room Checklist

Ideally, a child's room should be highly functional, teaming up a variety of elements, large and small. The checklist that follows highlights basic choices and considerations, and offers suggestions for conventional as well as novel decorating approaches.

BEDS

Beds for infants include bassinets, portable cribs, and full-size cribs—the last of these being the most expensive. It is important to choose a crib with a swing-down or swing-out gate so that caregivers don't have to bend over to pick up the baby, thereby risking back strain. Some cribs convert into toddler beds with guardrails to protect restless sleepers. Older children can graduate to single beds, bunk beds, loft/storage beds, or canopy beds. Trundle beds provide extra sleeping space for overnight guests or siblings sharing a room. Antique beds are appropriate as long as they are sturdy and free of lead paint (or of fumes from any paint remover or refinishing solution). *Do not lay an infant in an antique crib.* The slats may be spaced farther apart than is currently recommended, and the baby's head may get wedged between them.

STORAGE

The most important feature to consider when investing in children's storage is accessibility. Chests and interior closet fittings must be low enough so that children can reach their things and put them away easily. Drawers should have easy-to-grip handles and be free-gliding so that they can be opened and closed without a struggle. Deep slide-out baskets or cubbyholes are preferable to drawers for bulky clothing such as sweaters and sweatshirts. Low-hanging peg racks and clothes trees encourage children to hang up clothes that are worn frequently.

Portable multipurpose storage units are the best buy for children's rooms over the long term. Options include plastic or rubber bins with self-locking covers; freestanding steel, wood, or laminated shelving units; slide-out wire baskets; stackable plastic crates; and room dividers with large cubbyholes. Highly adaptable, these can hold anything from toys to books, can be rearranged as needed, and can be taken along to a new residence. Architectural storage units, though not readily portable, can be just as flexible in terms of what they contain. Options include built-in bookcases, window seats, and bed platforms with drawer or cupboard storage underneath and/or above. When choosing a storage unit for a child's room, examine it carefully for rough edges that could cause inadvertent injury, and make sure the unit is appropriate for the child's size and activities.

Work Surfaces & Desks

Smooth, washable work surfaces are practical for all ages. For younger children, a low table with matching chairs is perfect for coloring, looking at books, assembling picture puzzles, and playing with other toys. Even if children end up sprawled on the floor for some of these activities, having a table-and-chair set available that's just their size enhances their sense of comfort and self-confidence.

Older children need larger work surfaces. Adjustable student-size drafting tables are suitable for many hobbies, from sewing to model making. Desk surfaces should be deep enough to allow room for a personal computer or a textbook and notebook. It is important to provide plenty of drawers so that the top surface can be cleared of papers, supplies, and other equipment if necessary.

Lighting

If possible, the rooms of infants and young children should receive plenty of natural light throughout the day. (Be sure, however, to protect infants from direct rays.) A soft overhead light or several lamps around the room are ample for evening, as long as extra task lighting is placed at desks and hobby areas. A bedside lamp is a must for nighttime reading. Night-lights and hall lights can be kept on or off, depending on the sleeping patterns of the individual child.

Floors

The typical floor surfaces for bedrooms are wood, vinyl tile, and carpet. Wood and vinyl tile have smooth, hard surfaces that are easy to clean and are ideal for young children's play. Either one can be quite comfortable as long as the home's heating system is adequate and the floors are not cold to the touch. Plush pile carpeting introduces a touch of luxury to the bedroom that many people, including older children, prefer. In an old or drafty house, carpeting may be the best option.

Walls

Washable paints and wallpapers are the sensible choice for young children's rooms. Themed wallpapers with matching border prints can be quite attractive and fun, but be aware that they may limit rather than expand your decorating options. The child will certainly outgrow these wall treatments sooner than a solid-color paint finish. If you decide to commission a hand-painted mural, try to select a theme that has staying power. Large bulletin boards are a must for keeping track of artwork, photographs, greeting cards, report cards, party invitations, and other paper items. Remember to mount all bulletin boards at the child's eye level.

Sources

SOURCES

ARCHITECTS & INTERIOR DESIGNERS

(page 14)
Mary Webster Interiors
Princeton, NJ
(609) 921-9168

(pages 16, 173, right)
David Webster & Associates
New York, NY
(212) 924-8932

(page 19 and 46)
Peter Carlson Design, Inc.
Los Angeles, CA
(213) 969-8423

(page 22)
Scott Merrill, Architect
Vero Beach, FL
(407) 388-1600

(pages 26–27 and 28, bottom)
Gary Wolf, Architect
Boston, MA
(617) 742-7557

(pages 26, 34, 35)
Sarah Kaltman
New York, NY
(212) 366-9385

(page 27, bottom)
Barbara Southerland Designs
New York, NY
(212) 737-2233
Greenville, NC
(919) 830-1020

(page 29, top)
Vogt Group Associates
New Orleans, LA
(504) 528-9611

(pages 33, top and 145)
Robert DeCarlo Design Associates
New York, NY
(212) 245-2968

(page 33, bottom)
Josef Pricci Ltd.
New York, NY
(212) 570-2140

(page 38, top)
Christ Architects and Planners
Point Washington, FL
(904) 231-5538

(page 39)
J. Rolf Seckinger, Inc.
New York, NY
(212) 966-6644

(pages 40, 46–47, and 127, bottom)
Barbara Ostrom Associates, Inc.
Mahwah, NJ
(201) 529-0444
New York, NY
(212) 465-1808

(page 41)
The late Lowell Neas

(pages 42 and 208)
Michael Davis, Architect
London, England
(071) 407-6574

(pages 50, bottom, 229, and 242, top and bottom)
The late Rubén de Saavedra
Rubén de Saavedra
New York, NY
(212) 759-2892

(page 54)
Kehrt Shatken Sharon Architects
Princeton, NJ
(609) 921-1131

(page 58, top)
Gillian Temple Associates/ Fisons Horticultural Division
Bramford, Ipswich, England
(0473) 830492

(pages 60 and 156)
Mark Mack, Architect
Santa Monica, CA
(310) 822-0094
San Francisco, CA
(415) 777-5305

(page 61)
Raymond Jungles, ASLA, Inc.
Coconut Grove, FL
(305) 666-9299

(pages 63, 159, top, and 237, top)
Charles Riley
New York, NY
(212) 647-9128
Los Angeles, CA
(213) 931-1134

(page 65)
JTS Woodworks
Canyon Country, CA
(805) 251-0049

(page 66)
Seaside Union Architects
Santa Barbara, CA
(805) 963-4455

(page 67)
Ron Goldman, Architect
Malibu, CA
(310) 456-1831

(page 68)
Vincent Wolf Associates, Inc.
New York, NY
(212) 465-0590

(pages 69, right, 152, 154,
   and 171)
Hutton Wilkinson Interior
   Design
Los Angeles, CA
(213) 874-7760

(page 69, left)
Building Stone Institute
Purdys, NY
(914) 232-5725

(pages 71, 74, 76)
Warner Design Associates
San Francisco, CA
(415) 367-9033

(pages 72–73)
Berkus Group Architects
Santa Barbara, CA
(805) 963-8901

(page 77)
William Turnbull Associates
San Francisco, CA
(415) 986-3642

(page 78)
José Yturbe, Architect
Mexico City, Mexico

(page 79)
Marco Aldaco, Architect
Guadalajara, Mexico

(page 82)
Brian Murphy
Santa Monica, CA
(310) 459-0955

(page 86)
Mark Hutker & Associates
Vineyard Haven, MA
(508) 693-3340

(pages 88, top and 96, left)
Lyn Peterson
Motif Designs
New Rochelle, NY
(914) 633-1170

(page 90, bottom)
Debra Jones
Los Angeles, CA
(310) 476-1824

(pages 92 and 142, top)
Gary Wolf Architects, Inc.
Boston, MA
(617) 742-7557

(page 93)
Owen & Mandolfo,
   Architects
New York, NY
(212) 686-4576

(pages 95 and 143)
David Livingston Interiors
San Francisco, CA
(415) 392-2465
(page 96, right)
Carole and Marc Moscowitz
   Design
Sherman, CT
(203) 355-2500

(page 98)
Stephen Mallory &
   Associates
New York, NY
(212) 737-7171

(page 99)
C & J Katz Studio
Boston, MA
(617) 367-0537

(page 100)
Jacques Grange
Paris, France
(33–01) 4247–4734

(page 101, left)
Marge Young
Marge Young Interiors
East Northport, NY
(516) 368-5150

(page 102, right)
Ronald Bricke
Ronald Bricke & Associates
New York, NY
(212) 472-9006

(pages 103 and 160)
Barbara Barry, Inc.
Los Angeles, CA
(310) 276-9977

(pages 103 and 199)
Ann LeConey, Inc.
New York, NY
(212) 472-1265

(page 104)
Roy McMakin
Seattle, WA
(206) 323-6992

(page 107, top)
Diane Chapman
San Francisco, CA
(415) 346-2373

(page 107, bottom)
Ken Kelleher
Boston, MA
(617) 262-2060

(page 110)
Bettina Calderone Design
Sherman, CT
(203) 355-1995

(page 111, left)
Beverly Ellsley Interiors
Westport, CT
(203) 227-1157

(page 111, right)
Joe Ruggiero
Encino, CA
(818) 783-9256

(page 112)
Connie Beale
Connie Beale Interior
    Design
Greenwich, CT
(203) 629-3442

(pages 113 and 132, right)
Bruce Bierman
New York, NY
(212)243-1935

(page 114)
Florence Karasik
Shrewsbury, NJ
(908) 219-8700

(pages 115, left and 117,
    top)
Steven Ehrlich, Architect
Venice, CA
(310) 399-7711

(page 115, right)
Al Devido
New York, NY
(212) 517-6100

(page 117, bottom)
Lori Margolis
Commercial Design Group
Summit, NJ
(908) 277-2880

(page 118)
Ron Erenberg
Santa Monica, CA
(310) 459-1515

(page 119)
Jack Lowery & Associates,
    Inc.
New York, NY
(212) 734-1680

(page 120)
Cathleen Schmidtknecht
Oakland, CA
(510) 339-3397

(page 121)
Janet Lohman
Los Angeles, CA
(310) 471-3955

(page 122)
Allee Willis
Los Angeles, CA
(818) 985-6317

(page 124, bottom)
Vogue Furniture
Livonia, MI
(313) 422-3890

(page 125)
Peter Lawton
Design PLUS
Shrewsbury, MA
(508) 793-9670

(pages 126, 222, and 273)
Bonnie Siracusa
Great Neck, NY
(516) 482-3349

(page 127, top)
Nicholas Calder
Nicholas Calder Interior
New York, NY
(212) 861-9055

(page 128)
Schweitzer BIM
Los Angeles, CA
(213) 936-6163

(page 130)
Ed Cohen, ISID
Edward Cohen, Inc.
New York, NY
(212) 371-1554

James Justice, ISID
Beverly Hills, CA
(310) 285-0833

(page 132, left)
Ron Meyers
Los Angeles, CA
(213) 851-7576

(page 133)
Michael De Santis
Michael De Santis, Inc.
New York, NY
(212) 753-8871

(page 134)
David Rockwell and Jay
    Haverson
(formerly of
    Haverson/Rockwell
    Architects)
New York, NY
(212) 889-4182

(page 135)
JoAnne M. Kuehner
Naples, FL
(813) 434-6001

(page 136)
Thomas F. Kennedy, ASID
Saffron House Inc.
Boston, MA
(617) 737-8150

(page 137)
Nancy Mannucci, ASID
New York, NY
(212) 427-9868

(page 138, top)
Pereaux
Morristown, NJ
(201) 993-8255

(page 138, bottom)
Nancy Serafini
Homeworks
Wellesley, MA
(617) 237-7666

(page 139, top)
Carleton Varney
Dorothy Draper & Co., Inc.
New York, NY
(212) 758-2810

(page 139, bottom)
Arnelle Kase
Barbara Scavullo Design
San Francisco, CA
(415) 558-8774

(page 140)
Hugh Newell Jacobsen, FAI
Washington, D.C.
(202) 337-5200

(page 141, left)
Burr & McCallum Architects
Williamstown, MA
(413) 458-2121

(page 148)
Peter Moore & Associates
New York, NY
(212) 861-5544

(page 151)
JS Brown Design
Corona del Mar, CA
(714) 474-9233

(page 153)
Llanarte/Lemeau & Llana
New York, NY
(212) 675-5190

(page 155)
David Barrett, FASID
New York, NY
(212) 688-0950

(page 157)
Frank Gehry and Associates
Santa Monica, CA
(310) 828-6088

(page 158)
Roberto Redo
Eldorado 2000
Mexico City, Mexico

(page 159, bottom)
Ron Wagner/Timothy
    Vandamne
Ron Wagner Design
New York, NY
(212) 674-3070

(page 161)
Jarrett Hedborg
Studio City, CA
(818) 501-4239

(page 163)
The late Max Gordon

(pages 164 and 165)
Steve Arnold
West Hollywood, CA
(310) 657-1029

(page 168)
Patricia Crane Associates
Narberth, PA
(215) 668-4770

(page 169, top)
Ronnette Riley Architect,
    formerly Riley
        Henry Foster
New York, NY
(212) 594-4015

(page 170)
Connie Beale, Inc.
Greenwich, CT
(203) 629-3442

(page 173, left)
Nancy Mannucci, ASID,
    Inc.
New York, NY
(212) 427-9868

(page 174)
Design by Jeri Kelly
Bauhs & Dring
Chicago, IL
(312) 649-9484
Mural by Chuck Nitti
Chicago, IL
(312) 489-7716

(pages 175, top and 267,
    bottom)
Design by Ann Fitzpatrick
    Brown
Country Curtains
Stockbridge, MA
(413) 298-5565

(page 175, top)
Mural by Holly Fields
Hartwick, NY
(607) 293-6136

(page 176, top)
Marie Paul Pelle
Paris, France
(33–01) 4296–2414

(pages 176, bottom and
    181)
Barton Phelps Architect
Los Angeles, CA
(213) 934-8615

(page 177)
Piers Gough
London, England
(071) 253-2523

(page 178, top)
Dave Kent
Sante Fe, NM

(page 178, bottom)
Cory Buckner, AIA
Malibu, CA
(310) 457-9840

(page 180)
Frank Israel
Beverly Hills, CA
(310) 652-8087

(page 182)
Levy Design Partners
San Francisco, CA
(415) 777-0561

(page 183)
Steele + Associates
Arlington, VA
(804) 344-0066

(pages 184–185)
Moore Poe Architects
Arlington, VA
(703) 351-9100

(pages 186–187)
Kiss & Cathcart Architects
New York, NY
(212) 513-1711

(pages 188–189)
Nade Wijaya
Bali
(361) 32507

(page 190)
J. Rolf Seckinger, Inc.
Miami, FL
(305) 673-1566

(page 192)
Helen Cooper Associates
London, England
(071) 740-0711

(page 193)
Dan Carithers Design
    Consultant
Atlanta, GA
(404) 355-8661

(pages 194 and 204)
Ron Meyers
Los Angeles, CA
(213) 851-7576

(page 195)
Sam Botero Associates
New York, NY
(212) 935-5155

(page 197)
The late George
    Washington Smith
The Santa Barbara
    Historical Society
(805) 966-1601

(page 198)
Pavarini/Cole Interiors, Inc.
New York, NY
(212) 749-2047

(page 200, top)
Peggy Butcher
Ojai, CA
(805) 646-4218

(page 200, bottom)
Linda Marder Design
Los Angeles, CA
(310) 855-0635

(page 201)
Caron Girard Interiors
Princeton, NJ
(609) 924-1007

(page 202)
Kenneth Hockin Interior
    Decorator, Inc.
New York, NY
(212) 308-6261

(page 203, bottom)
Mark Hampton
New York, NY
(212) 753-4110

(page 205)
Larry Totah Architect
Los Angeles, CA
(213) 467-2927

(page 206)
Siskin/Valls, Inc.
New York, NY
(212) 752-3790

(page 207)
Carlson Chase Associates
Los Angeles, CA
(213) 969-8423

(page 209)
Jon Bok Furniture Designer
Los Angeles, CA
(213) 660-1544

(page 210, top)
Jeffrey Lincoln Interiors, Inc.
Locust Valley, NY
(516) 759-6100

(page 210, bottom)
Furniture by Alfred
    Cochrane
Ireland

(page 211)
Beverly Ellsley Collection of
    Handcrafted Cabinets
Westport, CT
(203) 454-0503

(pages 212, 256, and 264,
    top)
Suzanne Kelly
New York, NY
(212) 988-7721

(page 214)
Inter-IKEA Systems B.V.,
    IKEA U.S.
Plymouth Meeting, PA
(610) 834-0180

(pages 217 and 224)
Bill Caroll
Model Homes Interiors
Beltsville, MD
(301) 937-6145

(page 220, top)
Katherine Stephens
New York, NY
(212) 593-1109

(page 220, bottom)
Susan Black
Periwinkles
Medford, MA
(617) 623-1980

(pages 227 and 250)
Judith Cohen Interiors
Scarsdale, NY
(914) 723-3627

(page 230, bottom)
Marcia Conors
Growing Interior Design
Canton, MA
(617) 828-3213

(page 231)
Judith Slaughter
Alpharetta, GA
(404) 594-1768

(page 234)
Lisa Furse
Lisbon Interiors
Chicago, IL
(708) 295-1444

(page 236, top)
Michael Smith
Los Angeles, CA
(310) 278-9046

(page 236, bottom)
Ronald Bricke & Associates
New York, NY
(212) 472-9006

(pages 238 and 265)
Sara Olesker Ltd.
Chicago, IL
(312) 248-9100

(pages 239 and 269)
Joe Terrell
Los Angeles, CA
(213) 469-8044

(page 240, top)
D'Image Associates
Saddle River, NJ
(201) 934-5420
(page 240, bottom)
Izhar Patkin
New York, NY
(212) 254-3056

(page 243)
Susan Reichhart
S.H. Reichhart Interiors
Fallston, MD
(410) 557-9983

(page 244)
Claudia Skylar, Architect
Chicago, IL
(312) 935-0984

(page 246, left)
KHR Design
New York, NY
(212) 861-4805

(page 248)
Steven Ehrlich, Architect
Los Angeles, CA
(310) 828-6700

(page 249, top)
Susan Fredman
Lake Forest, IL
(708) 831-1419

(page 251)
Karen Berkemeyen
Greenwich, CT
(203) 869-8800

(page 253)
Adam Tihany
Tihany International
New York, NY
(212) 505-2360

(page 254)
Connie Driscoll Interior
    Design
Nantucket, MA
(617) 259-0878

(page 257, top)
Carole Kaplan
Two by Two Interior Design
Andover, MA
(508) 470-3131

(pages 257, bottom and
    272)
Debby Smith
Nantucket, MA
(508) 465-2435

(page 258)
Summer House for Kids
San Francisco, CA
(415) 383-6690

(page 264, bottom)
Peg Heron
Classic Galleries
Huntington, NY
(516) 427-1045

(page 266)
Fred Cannon, Jr.
New York, NY
(212) 753-5600

(page 271)
Terry Irvin
Dacula, GA
(404) 995-0165

(page 274)
Caledonian
Chicago, IL
(708) 446-6566

(page 275, left and right)
Vassa
The Vassa Group
Chicago, IL
(312) 664-5800

BUILDING PRODUCTS/TRADE ASSOCIATIONS

Brick Institute of America
11490 Commerce Park
    Drive
Reston, VA 22091
(703) 620-0010

Building Stone Institute
Box 507
Purdys, NY 10578
(914) 232-5725

California Redwood
    Association
405 Enfrente Drive
Suite 200
Novato, CA 94949
(415) 382-0662

Featherock, Inc.
20219 Bahama Street
Chatsworth, CA 91311
(818) 882-3888

Industrial Fabrics
    Association International
(awnings and architecture)
305 Cedar Street, Suite 800
St. Paul, MN 55101
(612) 222-2508

Maple Flooring
    Manufacturers
    Association
60 Revere Drive, Suite 500
Northbrook, IL 60062
(708) 480-9080

Marvin Windows and Doors
P.O. Box 100
Warroad, MN 56763
(800) 346-5128
(800) 552-1167 in
Minnesota

National Oak Flooring
Manufacturers
Association
P.O. Box 3009
Memphis, TN 38173
(901) 526-5016

Resilient Floor Covering
Institute
966 Hungerford Drive
Suite 12B
Rockville, MD 20850
(301) 340-8580

Southern Forest Products
Association
P.O. Box 641700
Kenner, LA 70064-1700
(504) 443-4464

Thompsons and Formby
(exterior and interior stains)
825 Crossover Lane
Memphis, TN 38117
(800) 367-6297

Tile Council of America
P.O. Box 326
Princeton, NJ 08542
(609) 921-7050

Velux Roof Windows and
Skylights
P.O. Box 5001
Greenwood, SC 29649
(803) 223-8780

Wolman Deck Care
Products
Kop-coat Inc.
1824 Koppers Building
436 Seventh Avenue
Pittsburgh, PA 15219
(800) 556-7737

SUNROOMS & CONSERVATORIES

Amdega/Machin
Conservatories
P.O. Box 713
Glenview, IL 60025
(708) 729-7212

Four Seasons Solar Products
5005 Veterans Memorial
Highway
Department C8
Holbrook, NY 11741
(800) 368-7732
(516) 563-4000

Prefabricated Gazebo
JTS Woodworks
18055 Beneda Lane
Canyon Country, CA
91351
(805) 251-0049

Photography Credits

© Otto Baitz: pp. 54 both, 55 both, 72, 73 both, 169, 186, 187 both
© Steven Brooke: pp. 22, 23 both, 29, 38 top, 61, 75
© Grey Crawford: pp. 115 left, 117 top, 118, 145 left, 239, 248, 269
© Derrick & Love: pp. 98, 119
© Daniel Eifert: pp. 50 bottom, 130, 198, 220 top, 229, 242 all
© Philip Ennis Photography: pp. 12, 14, 19, 24, 40, 41, 46, 56, 57 both, 100, 101 left, 102 right, 112, 116, 127 both, 131, 133, 138 both, 145 right, 170, 190, 195, 212, 219, 223 bottom, 236 bottom, 256, 261, 262, 264 top
Esto Photographics: © Peter Aaron: pp. 101 right, 245, © Otto Baitz: p. 225, © Mark Darley: pp. 97 right, 258, © Scott Frances: pp. 93, 141 left, 146, 238, 240 bottom, 246 left, 265, © Jeff Goldberg: pp. 247, 267 top

© Feliciano: pp. 11, 20, 80, 88 top, 96 left, 139 top, 249 bottom, 266
© Four Seasons Sunrooms: photos by Philip Ennis: pp. 48, 49
© Michael Garland: pp. 51, 65 both, 66, 90 top, 111 bottom, 151, 178 bottom, 200 top, 226, 237 bottom
© Gary Wolf Architects: p. 28 bottom
© Tria Giovan: pp. 15, 26, 27 top, 28 top, 34 both, 35, 44 both, 45, 52, 62, 88 bottom, 89, 97 left, 124 top, 132 right, 141 right, 159 top, 175 bottom, 211, 230 top, 237 top, 241 top
© David Glomb: pp. 176 bottom, 181
© John Glover: pp. 58 both, 64, 70 left
© Mick Hales: pp. 162, 179, 193, 196, 199, 201, 203 both
© David Henderson/Eric Roth Studio: pp. 257 bottom, 272
© David Hewitt/Anne Garrison: p. 37 top
© Nancy Hill: pp. 142 bottom, 168, 202, 227, 250, 252

© Inter-IKEA Systems B.V.: p. 214

© image/Dennis Krukowski: pp. 16, 25, 27 bottom, 33 bottom, 39, 68, 135, 137, 148, 153, 155, 158, 163 top, 166, 169 bottom, 172, 173 both, 175 top, 192, 206 both, 207, 210 both, 240 top, 267 bottom

© Balthazar Korab: pp. 124 bottom, 140

© Tim Lee: pp. 96 right, 110, 251

© Jennifer Levy: pp. 105, 113, 129

© David Livingston: pp. 30 left and right, 31, 43, 70 right, 71, 74, 76, 77, 85, 95, 107 top, 120, 139 bottom, 143, 144

© Mark Lohman: p. 121

© Marianne Majerus: pp. 47, 53, 59, 163 bottom

© Colin McRae: pp. 178 top, 182 both

© Michael Mundy: p. 236 top

© Randy O'Rourke: p. 176 top

© Peter Paige: pp. 50 top, 117 bottom, 159 bottom, 253

© Robert Perron: pp. 246 right, 260

© Prakosh Patel: pp. 183 both, 184, 185

© Eric Roth: pp. 7, 86, 92, 99, 107 bottom, 125, 136, 220 bottom, 221 all, 230 bottom, 254, 257 top, 259, 270

© Bill Rothschild: pp. 2, 5, 33 top, 69 right, 111 left, 114, 126, 218, 222, 223 top, 264 bottom, 273

© J. Brough Schamp/TAB Stock: p. 243

© Schulenburg/The Interior World: pp. 228, 232, 233, 235, 241 bottom, 268

© Ernest Silva/FPG International: p. 255

© Ron Solomon/TAB Stock: pp. 217, 224

© Tim Street-Porter: pp. 32, 38 bottom, 42, 60, 63, 67, 69 left, 78, 79, 82, 90 bottom, 103, 104, 106, 122, 128, 132 left, 152, 154, 156, 157, 160, 161, 164, 165, 167, 171, 177, 180, 188, 189, 191, 194, 197, 200 bottom, 204, 205, 208, 209

© Brian Vanden Brink: p. 8

© Peter Vanderwarker: pp. 36, 37 bottom; Peter Vanderwarker/Gary Wolf Architects: p. 142 top

© Jessie Walker & Associates: pp. 17, 91, 94, 102 left, 108, 174 both, 234, 244, 249 top, 274, 275 all

© Paul Warchol: pp. 115 right, 134

Index